Appearances of
the Son of God Under
the Old Testament

*With Quotes from the Fathers and Reformers
on Christ in the Old Testament*

John Owen (1616-1683)

Edited and Compiled
by Douglas Van Dorn

Appearances of the Son of God Under the Old Testament

With Quotes from the Fathers and Reformers on Christ in the Old Testament

John Owen (1616-1683)

Edited and Compiled by Douglas Van Dorn

Waters of Creation Publishing
Dacono, Colorado

First Published in 1668 as an exercitation in *Exercitations on the Epistle to the Hebrews, I* (London: Printed by Robert White for Nathaniel Ponder). More recently in *An Exposition of the Epistle to the Hebrews*, ed. W. H. Goold, vol. 18, Works of John Owen (Edinburgh: Johnstone and Hunter, 1854), reprinted by The Banner of Truth.

Cover Design: Doug, Breanna, and Alesha Van Dorn

ISBN: 978-0-9862376-4-5 (Waters of Creation Publishing)

Contents

Other Books by Waters of Creation

Waters of Creation: A Biblical-Theological Study of Baptism (2009)
Galatians: A Supernatural Justification (2012)
Giants: Sons of the Gods (2013)
Covenant Theology: A Reformed Baptist Primer (2014)
From the Shadows to the Savior: Christ in the Old Testament (2015)
The Unseen Realm: Q & A Companion (2016)
Five Solas (2019)

For more information, articles, radio shows, and broadcasts go to: dougvandorn.com

Editor's Introduction

Reason for This Series

I am convinced, after studying the topic of Christ in the Old Testament in some depth for the last several years, and having lived in modern conservative Reformed and Evangelical Christian circles for nearly 50 years, that too many Christians (past and present) far too often presuppose and/or superimpose a kind of Unitarian grid upon the OT. This is a very Liberal way of reading the Scripture, out of line with orthodox Christian teaching throughout history.

It isn't that this is done malevolently, for these same Christians often do see Christ in the OT in one way or another. I am not talking about a Christianity that outright denies the deity of Jesus. In fact, I'm talking about a Christianity that loves him as the *Theanthropos*—The God-man. It isn't that this is done deliberately either. At least, not usually. I would say it is more of a subconscious decision. We speak about Christ being there in type and shadow, but to say that he was actually there—*in person?* This is a hard pill for many to swallow. I had more than one professor in my conservative Baptist schooling tell the students that to see Christ or a Trinity actually there, as if any of the human authors could have deliberately written about these things when they wrote the OT books, was reading the NT back into the Old. It was eisegesis, not exegesis.

In this way, too many of us presuppose that the Jewish church did not, indeed *could not* have known the Christ to write about him actually being present in their midst. He simply wasn't there among them. At best, only the Father was. Yet, somehow, we think, they could foresee his coming. But this is a strange oxymoron, because that would seem to itself presuppose that they knew he already existed, if the Messiah they prophesied about was truly God. But if they knew he already existed, why couldn't he have known them or made himself known to them? Nevertheless, at the end of the day when we ask questions like *Job knew his Redeemer* (Job 19:25) *to be Christ?* Or *Solomon comprehended the Son of a Father who has ascended to heaven* (Prov 30:4) *was Christ?* Or *Abraham believed God* (Gen 15:6), *whom he knew to be Christ?* Not possible is a very common answer to hear.

As a case in point, there is an ancient manuscript variant in Jude 5 where one family of texts say "Jesus" lead Israel in the Exodus, while another family reads the "Lord" did it. Apparently, this discussion has been around for a long, long time. Some scribe was asking the same question: *Jude could call the Savior of the Exodus "Jesus?"* Not possible. So he changed "Jesus" to "Lord." The renowned NT scholar Bruce Metzger ran into the same skepticism I have run into in conservative circles on this very same variant when he was working on his *Textual Commentary on the Greek New Testament* in a committee with a bunch of other scholars. He wrote, "A majority of the Committee was of the opinion that the [Jesus] reading was difficult to the point of impossibility."[1]

Why? Because we presuppose it, that's why. Therefore, any OT text you can think of where a Christian has argued that we see the Trinity or Christ ("Holy, Holy, Holy" or "Let us make man in our image") must be dismissed out of hand.

This Work and Its Place in this Series

The work before you is a volume in the series: Christ in All Scripture, by Waters of Creation Publishing. At present, this series consists or will consist of the following volumes:

---

[1] Bruce Manning Metzger, United Bible Societies, *A Textual Commentary on the Greek New Testament, Second Edition a Companion Volume to the United Bible Societies' Greek New Testament (4th Rev. Ed.)* (London; New York: United Bible Societies, 1994), 657.

- *A Dissertation Concerning the Angel who is called the Redeemer and Other Select Passages* by Peter Allix
- *Appearances of the Son of God Under the Old Testament* by John Owen
- *The Worship of the Lord Jesus Christ in the Old Testament* by Gerard De Gols
- *The Angel of the LORD in Early Jewish, Christian, and Reformation History*, a compilation of Allix, Owen, and De Gols
- *Christ in the Old Testament: Promised, Patterned, and Present* by Douglas Van Dorn
- *Jesus: Who, What, Where, When, Why?* by Douglas Van Dorn

It serves as either a supplement or stand-alone book. As a supplement, it belongs with the forthcoming book by Matt Foreman and Douglas Van Dorn on the Angel of the LORD. Matt and I were simply not able to put all the material in that volume that we wanted, and the present book fills a needed gap in that it gives a detailed treatment of the Angel by one of the most respected Puritans in history.

The work presented here is an *exercitation*, by John Owen. An exercitation is a kind of preliminary practice to understanding the book of Hebrews and the person of Jesus Christ that Owen printed in the first volume of his commentary on that book. He called it "Promises of the Messiah Vindicated." His treatment of the Angel deals with, among other things, significant passages in Scripture, Philo, and the Targums.

Following the exercitation are two lengthy sections of quotations on the Angel of the LORD. The first is quotations from the Church Fathers; the second is quotations from the Reformers. These go through the Scripture, beginning with Adam, looking at various places in the OT where the Angel has been understood to be Christ.

I would recommend Owen's *Exercitation* and the attached quotations in this volume for anyone particularly needing or desiring to see the orthodoxy of this understanding of the Angel of the LORD. The antiquity of the view combined with the pedigree of those espousing it should be deeply considered when coming to your own conclusions. As for John Owen, it is difficult to find a more celebrated or respected Puritan. His views are held in great esteem and should carry no little authority as a pastor/scholar of unsurpassed reputation, reverence, and respect.

John Owen

Let's look at our author. John Owen was born in 1616 in Stadhampton, Oxfordshire England. Though of Welsh descent, he became one of the best known of all the English Puritans. He was married to Mary Rooke, who gave him 11 children, 10 of which died in infancy. He became pastor at Coggeshall in Essex but found himself also influencing politics thanks to his friendship with Oliver Cromwell, through whom he eventually found himself dean of Christ Church Cathedral in Oxford. He published the *Exercitations* in 1668 along with his comments on the early parts of Hebrews. Owen died in 1683.[2]

A Note on Editing

I have completely revised the English as it is found in Owen's *Works* (most recently published by The Banner of Truth). I have taken some liberties in order to shorten and make the work more accessible to people who might not ordinarily be drawn to this man whose works are unusually difficult to read (both for the depth of content and the often-convoluted English). All original margin notes have been retained as footnotes, but I have added several notes to help in understanding.

My hope is that being confronted by Owen and a myriad of Fathers and Reformers will help settle the reader into a sure and certain confidence as to the much questioned fact that the OT church did in fact know and worship the Lord Jesus Christ, especially when he came to them as the Angel of the LORD, who is, in fact, the Second Person of the Holy Trinity, the Son pre-incarnate, the Redeemer whom those people

---

[2] Allow me to recommend a new short biography: *John Owen: The Prince of Puritans*, Wrath and Grace Biographies (Columbus, GA: Wrath and Grace Publishing, 2019), by my friend Luke Walker.

before Messiah came, knew, trusted in, and worshiped as Yahweh-God.

A more important topic is difficult to discern, especially in days like ours when the OT has fallen on such hard times. Reading others who have gone before us talk about him in such clear, profound, and direct ways should be a balm to the soul of any Christian and a powerful apologetic against unbelief.

Doug Van Dorn
October 2019

——— ——— ———

Promises of the Messiah Vindicated

JOHN OWEN

EXERCITATION X
APPEARANCES OF THE SON OF GOD
UNDER THE OLD TESTAMENT

Overview:

Ends of the promises and prophecies concerning the Messiah—Other ways of his revelation; of his offering, by sacrifices; of his divine person, by visions. 2. What is meant in the Targums by Memra Debar, the Word of God—The expression qol Yahweh, first used in Gen 3:8. Apprehensions of the ancient Jews about the Word of God; of the philosophers—Application of the expression "the Logos of God" to the Son, by John—Expressions of Philo—Among the Mohammedans Christ called the Word of God—Intention of the Targumists vindicated. 3. How the Voice walked—Aben Ezra refuted, and R. Jona—The appearance of the second Person unto our first parents. 4. Gen 18:1–3—God's appearance, and the Suddenness of it. 5. Who appeared. 6. The occasion of it. 7. Reflection of Aben Ezra on some Christian expositors countered—A trinity of persons not proved from this place—Distinct persons proved—No created angel representing the person of God called Jehovah—Gen 19:24, "From the LORD*"—Exceptions of Aben Ezra and Jarchi removed—Appearance of the second Person. 8. Gen 32:24, 26–30. 9. Occasion of this vision. 10. The Person; in appearance a man; 11. In office, an angel, Gen 48:16; 12, 13. In nature, God, Gen 32:26, 30, Hos 12:5, who it was that appeared. 14. Ex 3:1–6, 14—God appeared. 15. Ex 19:18–20—Who gave the law—Not a created angel—The ministry of angels, how used therein. 16, 17. Ex 23:20–23—Different angels promised—The Angel of God's presence, who. 18, 19. Josh 5:13–15—Captain of the Lord's host described. 20. Sense of the ancient church concerning these appearances; 21. Of the Jews. 22. Opinion of Nachmanides. 23. Tanchuma—Talmud—Fiction of the angel rejected by Moses, accepted by Joshua—Sense of it. 24. Metatron, who—Derivation of the name.*

1. We have seen how often God instructed the church of old by his prophets in the knowledge of the person, office, and work of the Messiah. He did this, partly, so that nothing might be lacking in the faith and comfort of believers, according to a fitting quantity that equaled the amount of light and grace that it was his good pleasure to give them before his actual coming in human flesh. It was also partly so that his righteous judgments that came from the rejection and ruin of those who obstinately refused him, might, because of their conviction, be justified and rendered glorious. These promises and predictions were not the

only means by which God would manifest and reveal him to their faith.

There are two things about the Messiah which are the pillars and foundation of the church. The one is his *divine nature*; and the other, his work of mediation in the *atonement* for sin, which he made by his suffering and sacrifice of himself.

He declared these two things to those whom, according to the promise, looked forward to his coming. He did this in two special ways or means that were graciously designed by God. The second of these was that the *worship* which he instituted, and the various *sacrifices* which he appointed to be observed in the church, would be types and representations of the one perfect sacrifice which he would offer in the fullness of time. The explanation and application of this means of instruction is the main purpose and reason the apostle Paul wrote his Epistle to the Hebrews.

The other way, which concerns his divine person, was through those *visions* and *appearances* of the Son of God (who is the head of the church) which were graciously given to the fathers under the Old Testament. These, as they are directly suited to our purpose, in our inquiry after the prophecies of the advent of the Messiah, are also eminently useful for the conviction of the Jews. For in them we shall demonstrate that a revelation was made of a *distinct person* in the Godhead, who in a peculiar manner managed all

the matters of importance in the church after the entrance of sin. Here, also, according to our proposed
method, we will inquire into what light was given regarding this truth that was then received by any of the
Jewish masters, who also aptly demonstrate what confusion they are driven to, when they seek to evade the
evidence that is in their own ancient writings.

2. There is frequent mention in the Targumists[3]
of the *Memra Debar*, "The Word of the Lord." It first
occurs in them at the first appearance of a divine person after the sin and fall of Adam (Gen 3:8). The
words of the original text are, "*And they heard the voice
of the LORD God walking in the garden.*" The participle
"walking" may be linked as much to the "the voice,"
as to "the LORD God." And although "the voice"
most commonly signifies the outward voice and
sound of something, yet when applied to God, it frequently denotes "his almighty power." It is through
this power that he affects whatever he pleases. Thus,
in Psalm 29:3–9, those things are ascribed to this "*voice
of the LORD,*" which elsewhere are assigned to "*the
word of his power*" (Heb 1:3).

Now, all these mighty works of creation or prov-
idence, which are assigned to this "voice of the

---

[3] A Targum is essentially a Jewish paraphrase of an OT book like
Genesis. In some ways they can be comparable to anything from
the NIV to The Message Bible. Some Targums are little more than
good translations. Others will add substantial oral tradition to help
illuminate a particular passage. The Targums are found in the language of Aramaic.

LORD," or to "the word of his power," or "his powerful word" are immediately brought to pass by the essential Word of God (John 1:3, Col 1:16), which was with God "*in the beginning*," or at the creation of all things (John 1:1, 2) as his eternal wisdom (Pro 8:22–26) and power. This expression, therefore, of "the voice of the LORD" may also denote the Word of God that is God, the essential Word of God, the Person of the Son: for here our first parents heard this "Word walking in the garden" before they heard the outward sound of any voice or words whatsoever. For God did not speak to them until after this (Gen 3:9) when, "*The LORD God called unto Adam, and said to him…*"

Some of the Jews take notice of this change of the appearance of God. So, the author of *Tseror Hammor*, Sect. *Bereshith*,[4] "Before they sinned, they saw the glory of the blessed God speaking with them; but after their sin they only heard his voice walking." God now dealt differently with them than he did before. And the Chaldee paraphrast [that is the Targum], observing that some special presence of God is expressed in the words, renders them, "And they heard the voice *of the Word* of the Lord God walking in the garden." All the Targums read this way. The Jerusalem Targum begins the next verse by saying, "And *the Word of*

---

[4] Owen refers here to a commentary on the Pentateuch written by Abraham Saba in 1523. See the Glossary and Works Cited at the end of the book for this and other references in this exercitation.

the Lord God called to Adam." And this expression they afterwards make use of in too many places to count,[5] and this in such a way as to plainly denote a distinct person in a Godhead. That this also was their intent is plain, because about the time of the writing of the first of those Targums, it was usual among them to express their conceptions of the Son of God by the name of "the Word of God," which is what *Memra Debar* means.

Thus, Philo express it in *The Confusion of Languages*, "If anyone is not yet worthy to be called the son of God, yet strives to be conformed to his first-begotten Word, the most ancient angel, the archangel with many names; for he is called the Beginning, the Name of God, the Man according to the image of God, the Seer of Israel." How perfectly these things speak to the mysteries revealed in the Gospel is a thing we will discuss elsewhere. Here I only observe how he calls that Angel who appeared to the fathers, and that sometimes in human form, the Word—"The first-begotten Word."

He expresses himself again in the same way to the same end: "For if we are not yet able to be called the sons of God, let us become like his eternal image, the most sacred Word; for that most ancient Word is the

---

[5] For the curious reader, both Peter Allix and Gerard De Gols go to great lengths to uncover many more references here than Owen did. We are publishing both of their works on Christ in the Old Testament in this same series as Owen's Exercitation.

image of God." How these things fit in with our apostle concerning Jesus Christ (Col 1:15–18, Heb 1:3) is easily discerned. This conception of theirs was so well approved by the Holy Ghost as being a thing fitting to the mind of God, that John in the beginning of his Gospel declares the eternal deity of Christ by using this name of The *Logos* ("the Word"), that is *Memra Debar*, "the Word of God." "*The Word was with God, and the Word was God*" (John 1:1). He alludes here to the story of the first creation, where God is described as making all things by his word; for he said of everything, "*Let it be*," and it was made (as the psalmist says it, "*He spoke, and it was done; he commanded, and it stood fast.*" Ps 33:9). This, the Psalmist fully declares in verse 6, "*By the word of the LORD were the heavens made, and all the host of them by the breath of his mouth.*" John thus teaches that all things were made by this Word of God (John 1:3). In the Chaldee, this is elsewhere also assigned to this Word. Where "the Word" is not mentioned in the original Hebrew (such as in Isa 45:12 or 48:13), it is in the Targums, just as it is discussed by Peter himself (2Pe 3:5), for the very reason that he might ascribe the work of the redemption of the church to this Word of the Lord, which was admitted in the church of the Jews. That place, among others, is straight to the point. Consider Hosea 1:7 where the prophet says, "*I will save them by the LORD their God*," the Targumist reads, "I will save (or redeem) them *by the Word* of the LORD their God;" the Word, the Redeemer.

It is not unworthy of consideration that the wisest and most contemplative of the philosophers of old had many notions about "the eternal Word," which was to them "the formative or creative power of the universe." To this end, many sayings have been observed and might be reported out of Plato, with his followers Amelius, Chalcidius, Proclus, Plotinus, and others. These expressions are imitated by our own writers, such as Justin Martyr, Clement, Athenagoras, Tatian, and many more. It is even so among the Mohammedans. This is the name that they give to Jesus in their Koran, "*The Word of God.*" This is how prevalent this notion of the Son of God has been in the world.

There are the words of Ezekiel, "*I heard the voice of their wings, as the voice of the Almighty*" (Ezek 1:24). These are rendered by the Targumist, "as the voice *from the face* of the Almighty." Some copies of the LXX[6] render them by "the voice *of the Word*," that is of God, who was represented in that vision, as shall be made clear. Some would put another sense on that expression of the Targumists, as though it intended nothing but God himself. Instances of this use have been observed. For example, Ecclesiastes 8:17, "If a

---

[6] LXX = The Greek Septuagint. This is the 3rd–2nd cent. B.C. translation of the OT Hebrew Bible into Koine Greek by seventy [hence LXX] Jewish scribes living in Alexandria, Egypt.

wise man say '*in his word*,'" that is, say in himself, or Genesis 6:6, "It repented the LORD *in his word*." Also, Ruth 3:8 makes some think this, "As did Phaltiel the son of Laish, who placed his sword *between his word* and Michal the daughter of Saul, the wife of David."

But there are a couple of things to say about this. 1. The former places do not use the word *mymr* [*memra*] which is peculiar to the sense we are arguing for. 2. The Targums on the Hagiographa are a late post-Talmudical endeavor, made in imitation of those of Onkelos and Ben Uzziel, when the Jews had both lost all sense of their old traditions and use of the Chaldee language, except for what they had learned from those former paraphrases. Nothing, therefore, can be concluded as to the intention of the Targumists in these words. But they can have no other sense in Psalm 110:1, "The LORD said in (or "to") his Word;" which replaces, "*to my Lord*," as in the original.

3. The Jews discern that "walking" relates in this place immediately to "the voice," and not to "the LORD God." They therefore try to render a reason for that kind of expression. So Aben Ezra on the place gives instances where a voice or sound in its progress is said to walk, such as Exodus 19:19, "*The voice of the trumpet went and waxed strong*;" and Jeremiah 46:22, "*The voice shall go like a serpent*." But these examples do not touch these under consideration; for although *halak* ("to walk") may sometimes express the

progression or increase of a voice, yet it does so only where it is hinted to have begun before. But here, nothing is spoken by God until after Adam had heard this Word of God walking. And therefore Rabbi (R.) Jona,[7] cited by Aben Ezra, would apply "walking" to Adam, "he heard the voice of God *as he was himself walking in the garden.*" The words of the text and context sufficiently verify the absurdity of this fiction. It is therefore most probable that in the great changes that were now coming upon the whole creation, with mankind being cast out of covenant, the serpent and the earth being cursed, and a way of recovery for the elect of God being revealed, he by whom all things were made, and by whom all were to be renewed that were brought back to God, did in a special and glorious way appear to our first parents, as he in whom this whole dispensation centered, and to whom it was committed. After the promise given, he appeared "in a human shape," to instruct the church in the mystery of his future incarnation, and under the name of Angel, to foreshadow his office as he was sent to it and was employed in it by the Father. So here, before the promise, he discovered his distinct glorious person, as the eternal Voice or Word of the Father.

4. Genesis 18:1–3. "*And the* LORD *appeared unto him* (Abraham) *in the plains of Mamre: and he sat in the*

---

[7] Rabbi Jonah (4th century). Palestinian amora who was the leading rabbinical authority in the 4th amoraic generation.

tent door in the heat of the day; and he lifted up his eyes and looked, and, lo, three men stood by him: and when he saw them, he ran to meet them from the tent door, and bowed himself toward the ground, and said, 'My Lord, if now I have now found favor in your sight...'" The Jews, in Bereshith Ketanna,[8] say that this appearance of God to Abraham was three days after his circumcision. Because he was still sore and was not yet recovered, he sat in the door of his tent. Thus, God came to visit him in his sickness. But the reason for his sitting in the door of the tent is given in the text, namely, because it was *"as in"* (or *"about"*) *"the heat of the day."* The day growing hot was the very opposite of the time God appeared to Adam, which was *"in the cool air of the day."* Just as when God comes to curse and nothing can refresh the creature, even though its own nature is suited for the cool of the day, it shall wither nevertheless wither; so also when he comes to bless, nothing shall hinder the influence of that blessing upon his creatures, even if a thing like the heat of the day is found to be troublesome or disconcerting.

   5. *"He lifted up his eyes and looked, and, behold, three men stood by him."* The title is, *"The* LORD *appeared to him;"* and the narrative is, *"Behold, three men stood by him."* The LORD, therefore, was among them. This seems to be a sudden appearance that was made to

---

[8] Bereshith Ketanna is one of many ways the midrashim on the Pentateuch are referred to by the Jews.

him. He saw them suddenly standing by him; he looked up and saw them, and this satisfied him that it was a heavenly apparition.

6. The business of God with Abraham at this time was to renew to him the promise of the blessing Seed, and to confine it to his posterity by Sarah. This was because he had grown despondent and began to desire that Ishmael might be his heir. Joined to this work of mercy was the declaration of an eminent *vindictive justice*, where God would set forth an example to all coming generations, in the destruction of Sodom and Gomorrah. Both of these are the proper works of him on whom the care of the church was in a special way incumbent. All whose blessedness depended on that promise, and to whom the rule of the world, the present and future judgment thereof, is committed, needed to see the person of the Son. And hence, in the overthrow of those cities, he who will be their judge is said to set forth an example of his future dealings with all the ungodly (2Pe 2:6).

7. Aben Ezra reflects with scorn on the Christians from this place. Because three men are said to appear to Abraham and he calls them, *"My Lord,"* some would prove the tri-personality of God. "Because of the appearance of three men, God is three, and he is one, and they are not separated or divided." How does he answer what they say? "Behold, they forget that two angels came to Sodom" (in other words, two of

those who appeared were angels and nothing more). But if any Christians have taken these three persons to have been the three persons of the Trinity,[9] it is an easy thing to demonstrate their mistake with instances of his own and companion's wicked curiosities and errors.

It is true, a Trinity of Persons in the Godhead cannot be proved from this place, seeing that one of them is expressly called Jehovah, and the other two, in distinction from him, are said to be angels (this and no more, Gen 19:1). Yet a distinction of persons in the Deity, although not the precise number of them, is certainly demonstrable. For it is evident that the one of the three who spoke to Abraham, and to whom he made his supplication for the sparing of Sodom, was Jehovah, "*the Judge of all the earth*" (18:22–33). And yet all the three were sent for the work, that one being the Prince and Head of the embassy; as he who is Jehovah is said to be sent by Jehovah (Zech 2:8-9).[10]

Neither is there any ground for the late exposition of this and similar places, namely, that a created angel representing the person of God both speaks and acts in his name and is called Jehovah [Yahweh]. This

---

[9] This Interpretation became common in in the fourth and fifth century in the Christian Church, though prior to that, the Fathers tended to see only one of the three as God—God the Son.

[10] Modern scholars have noted certain two-powers texts (as the rabbis called them) which seem to show not one but two Yahwehs. This passage in Zechariah is drawing upon that kind of tradition, as will be seen below when Owen cites Genesis 19:24.

is an invention crafted to evade the appearances of the Son of God in the Old Testament. It is against the interpretation of all antiquity. And it is contrary to any reason or instance produced to make it good. The Jews, indeed, say that they were three angels, because of the threefold work they were employed in; for they say, "No more than one angel is at any time sent about to the same work." So, one of these was to renew the promise to Abraham; another, to deliver Lot; and the third, to destroy Sodom. But this is a rule of their own making, and evidently false. This is easily proven from places like Genesis 32:1-2 or 2 Kings 6:17. Besides, in the story itself it is obvious that they were all engaged in the same work, one as Lord and Prince, the other two as his ministering servants.

This is further clarified in that expression of Moses, "*The LORD rained upon Sodom and upon Gomorrah brimstone and fire from the LORD out of heaven*" (Gen 19:24). Here, the Targum reads, "from before the Lord," or "the face of the Lord." Aben Ezra answers that this is the elegance of the language, but the sense of it is, "from himself;" and this gloss some of the late critics embrace. There are instances collected by Solomon Jarchi to confirm this sense:

- The words of Lamech (Gen 4:23): "*Hear my voice, you wives of Lamech*," not "my wives."
- The words of David (1 Kings 1:33): "*Take with you the servants of your lord*," not "my servants."

- The words of Ahasuerus to Mordecai (Esther 8:8): "*Write for the Jews in the king's name*," not "in my name."

But the difference of these from the words under consideration is wide and evident. In all these places the persons are introduced speaking of themselves and describe themselves either by their names or offices. But in this place, it is Moses who speaks of the Lord, and he had no reason or purpose to repeat "from the Lord," except to hint at the distinct persons to whom that name, denoting the nature and self-existence of God, was proper. One appeared on the earth; the other manifested his glorious presence in heaven.

Rashi, observing somewhat more in this expression, does not content himself with his supposed parallel places; but adds, that the "house of judgment" is to be understood. He then gives this as a rule, "Every place where it is said, '*And the* LORD,' he and his house of judgment are intended"! as if God had a Sanhedrin in heaven, an imagination which they have invented to avoid the expressions which testify to a plurality of persons in the Deity. There is therefore in this place an appearance of God in a human shape, where one distinct person in the Godhead, who now represented himself to Abraham in the form and shape, where later he would dwell among men, would be "*made flesh*" from Abraham's seed. This was the chief way that Abraham "*saw his day and rejoiced*;" which proves his *pre-existence* before his incarnation, more than just the promise of his coming (John 8:56, 58). This was a solemn introduction to his taking of flesh, a revelation of his divine nature and person, and a pledge of his coming in human nature to converse with men.

8. Genesis 32:24, 26–30. "*And Jacob was left alone. And a man wrestled with him until the breaking of the day … Then he said, 'Let me go, for the day has broken.' But Jacob said, 'I will not let you go unless you bless me.' And he said to him, 'What is your name?' And he said, 'Jacob.' Then he said, 'Your name shall no longer be called Jacob, but Israel, for you have striven with God and with men, and have prevailed.' Then Jacob asked him, 'Please tell me your name.' But he said, 'Why is it that you ask my name?' And there he blessed him. So Jacob called the name of the place Peniel, saying, 'For I have seen God face to face, and yet my life has been delivered.'*"

This story is twice reflected upon in the Scripture after the fact. Once is by Jacob himself, "*And he blessed Joseph and said, 'The God before whom my fathers Abraham and Isaac walked, the God who has been my shepherd all my life long to this day, the angel who has redeemed me from all evil, bless the boys'*" (Genesis 48:15-16). The other is by the prophet Hosea, "*In the womb he took his brother by the heel, and in his manhood he strove with God. He strove with the angel and prevailed; he wept and sought his favor. He met God at Bethel, and there God spoke with us—the LORD, the God of hosts, the LORD is his memorial name*"

(Hos 12:3–5). In the first place he is called a "man" ("a man wrestled with him," Gen 32:24). In the second, Jacob calls him an "Angel" ("The Angel which redeemed me," 48:16). In the third, he is expressly said to be "God, the LORD God of hosts" (Hos 12:3, 5).

9. Jacob was now passing with his whole family into the land of Canaan, to take possession of it by virtue of the promise on the behalf of his posterity. At the entrance of it he is met by his greatest adversary, with whom he had a severe contest about the promise and the inheritance itself. This was his brother Esau, who was coming against him with a power which he was in no way able to withstand. He feared that he would utterly destroy both he himself and his children (Gen 32:11). In the promise which brought about that dreadful contest, the blessed Seed, with the whole church-state and worship of the Old Testament, was included. This made it the greatest controversy, and had the utmost weight depending on it, of any contest that ever was among the sons of men. Thereupon, to settle Jacob's right, to preserve him with his title and interest, he who was principally concerned in the whole matter did here appear to him; some special facts of this manifestation of himself may be observed.

10. First, he appeared in the form of "a man." "*A man wrestled with him.*" He is called a man because of his shape and his actions. He "wrestled." R. Menachem in Rashi says literally, "he dusted." This, he

says, is the sense of *'abaq*, for "*they stirred up the dust with their feet,*" as men do when they wrestle; or, as he would have it in allusion to another word to signify "*the closing with their arms,*" to cast one another down, as is the manner of wrestlers. A great contention is denoted, and an appearance in the form of a man, further manifested by his "*touching the socket of Jacob's thigh.*"

11. Second, he is called an "*Angel*" by Jacob himself. "*The Angel that redeemed me*" (Gen 48:16). This was the greatest danger that Jacob was ever in, and this he remembers in his blessing of Joseph's children, praying that they may have the presence of this Angel with them, who preserved him all his life, and delivered him from that imminent danger from his brother Esau. And he calls him, "*The Angel the Redeemer;*" which is the name of the promised Messiah, as the Jews grant, "*And the Goël* (the 'Redeemer') *shall come to Zion*" (Isa 59:20). He is also expressly called "*The Angel*" in Hosea 12:4.

12. Third, this man in appearance, this angel in office, was in name and nature God over all, blessed forever. For, in the first place, Jacob prays solemnly to him for his blessing (Gen 32:26), and refuses to let him go, or to cease his appeals, until he had blessed him. He does so, he blesses him, and gives him a double pledge or token of it, in the touch of his thigh and change of his name; giving him a name to denote his prevailing with God—that is, with himself. From

this, Jacob concludes that he had "*seen God*," and calls the name of the place, "*The face of God*." In the second place, Genesis 48:16, besides that he invokes this Angel for his presence with and blessing on the children of Joseph,—which cannot regard any but God himself without gross idolatry—it is evident that "the Angel who redeemed him" (16) is the same with "*the God who fed him*," that is, the God of his fathers.

And this is all the more evident in the prophet. For with regard to this story of his power over the Angel, he says, "*He had power with God;*" and proves it, because "*he had power over the Angel, and prevailed.*" And he shows exactly how he prevailed. It was by "*weeping and making supplication to him;*" which he neither did nor lawfully might do to a created angel. And therefore some of the Jews apply these words, "*He wept and made supplication,*" to the Angel's desire for Jacob to let him go!—foolishly enough; and yet they are also followed by some late critics, who too often please themselves in their curiosities. Again, this Angel was he whom he found, or "*who found him, in Bethel;*" an account that we have in Genesis 28:10–22 and 35:1. Now, this was none other than he to whom Jacob made his vow, and entered into solemn covenant so that he should be his God. And therefore, the prophet adds expressly in the last place that it was "*the LORD God of hosts*" (Hos 12:5) whom he intended.

13. From what has been spoken, it is obvious that he who appeared to Jacob, with whom he earnestly wrestled, by tears and supplications, was God; and because he was sent as the angel of God, it must be some distinct person in the Godhead condescending to that office. Appearing in the form of a man, he represented his future assumption of our human nature. And in all this God instructed the church in the mystery of the person of the Messiah, who it was that they were to look for in the blessing of the promised Seed.

14. Exodus 3:1–6. "*Now Moses was keeping the flock of his father-in-law, Jethro, the priest of Midian, and he led his flock to the west side of the wilderness and came to Horeb, the mountain of God. And the angel of the LORD appeared to him in a flame of fire out of the midst of a bush. He looked, and behold, the bush was burning, yet it was not consumed. And Moses said, 'I will turn aside to see this great sight, why the bush is not burned.' When the LORD saw that he turned aside to see, God called to him out of the bush, 'Moses, Moses!' And he said, 'Here I am.' Then he said, 'Do not come near; take your sandals off your feet, for the place on which you are standing is holy ground.' And he said, 'I am the God of your father, the God of Abraham, the God of Isaac, and the God of Jacob.' And Moses hid his face, for he was afraid to look at God.*"

Here also have we expressed another glorious appearance of the Son of God. He who is revealed here is called "*Jehovah*" (4); and he affirms of himself that he is "*the God of Abraham*" (6); who also describes himself by the glorious name of "*I AM THAT I AM*" (14); in whose name and authority Moses dealt with Pharaoh in the deliverance of the people, and whom they were to serve on that mountain upon their coming out of Egypt; he whose "*merciful good-will*" Moses prays for (Dt 33:16). And yet he is expressly called an "Angel" (Ex 3:2), namely, the Angel of the covenant, the great Angel of the presence of God, in whom was the name and nature of God. He thus appeared so that the church might know and consider who it was that was to work out their spiritual and eternal salvation, that deliverance which he then would affect was a type and pledge. Aben Ezra would have the Angel mentioned in vs. 2 to be another from him who is called "God" (6). But the text will not tolerate any such distinction, but speaks of one and the same person throughout, without any alteration; and this was none other but the Son of God.

15. Exodus 19:18–20. "*Now Mount Sinai was wrapped in smoke because the LORD had descended on it in fire. The smoke of it went up like the smoke of a kiln, and the whole mountain trembled greatly. And as the sound of the trumpet grew louder and louder, Moses spoke, and God answered him in thunder. The LORD came down on Mount Sinai, to the top of the mountain. And the LORD called Moses to the top of the mountain, and Moses went up.*"

The Jews do well interpreting these words to be about the descent of God by way of the manifestation of his glory, rather than a change of place. Hence Aben Ezra interprets that expression, "*You have seen that I have talked with you from heaven*" (20:22). God was still in heaven when his glory was on the mount. Yet these words, "from heaven" refer to his descent, described earlier, rather than denote the place from which he spoke. For in giving the law, God "*spoke on earth*" (Heb 12:25). God did, in the glorious manifestation of his presence on mount Sinai, make use of the ministry of angels. The nature of the thing declares it, and the Scripture testifies to it (Ps 68:17). The voices, fire, trembling of the mountain, smoke, and noise of the trumpet, were all effected by them. So also was the forming of the words of the law conveyed to the ears of Moses and the people. Hence, the law is not only said to be received by them "*by the disposition* (or "*orderly ministries*") *of angels*" (Acts 7:53), and to be placed by them into the hand of Moses (Gal 3:19); but is also called "*the word spoken* (or "*pronounced*") *by angels*," that is, outwardly and audibly.

As to him who presided and ruled the whole action, some Christians think it was a *created angel*, representing God and speaking in his name. But if this is so, we have no certainty of anything that is affirmed in the Scripture. It may refer directly and immediately to God, yet we may, when we so please, substitute a *delegated angel* whenever we want; for in no place, not even in that concerning the creation of the world, is God himself more expressly spoken of than here in Exodus. Besides, the psalmist in the place mentioned affirms that when those chariots of God were on mount Sinai, Jehovah himself was in the midst of them. The Hebrews call this presence of God the *Kavod*, and the *Shekinah*, and the *Yeqar*; by which they understand a majestic and sanctifying presence. Indeed, it certainly fits him who is the "*brightness of the Father's glory, and the express image of his person,*" who was delegated to this work as the great Angel of the covenant, giving the law "*in the strength of the LORD, in the majesty of the name of the LORD his God.*"

16. Exodus 23:20–22. "*Behold, I send an angel before you to guard you on the way and to bring you to the place that I have prepared. Pay careful attention to him and obey his voice; do not rebel against him, for he will not pardon your transgression, for my name is in him. But if you carefully obey his voice and do all that I say, then I will be an enemy to your enemies and an adversary to your adversaries.*"

The Angel here promised is he who went in the midst of the people in the wilderness, whose glory appeared and was manifested among them. Moreover, another angel is promised to them in vs. 23, "*For my angel shall go before you, and bring you in to the Amorites … and I will cut them off.*" It is a ministering angel, to execute the judgment and vengeance of God upon the enemies of his people. That this angel of verse 23 is different from that of verse 20 appears from Exodus 33:2-3 compared with verses 13–16 of the same chapter. Verse 2, "*I will send an angel before you, and I will drive out the Canaanites, the Amorites...*"; which is the promise and the angel of 23:23. But he says, "*I will not go up among you*" (33:3), which he had promised to do in and by the Angel of 23:20-21, in whom his name was. From this the people feared evil tidings and mourned because of it (33:4). Now, God had not promised to go in their midst in any way other than by the Angel mentioned; with which both Moses and the people were abundantly satisfied. But whereas here he renews his promise of the ministry and assistance of the angel of 23:23, yet he denies them his own presence in the Angel of verse 20, for which Moses renews his request (33:13). To this God replies, "*My presence will go with you*" (14): concerning which presence, or face of God, or which Angel of his presence we must look at just a little bit more.

17. (1.) It is said to the people concerning him, "*Beware of him,*" or rather, "*Take heed to yourself before him,*"—before his face, in his presence (23:21). This is the caution that is usually given the people whenever reverence and awe is to be paid to the holiness of the presence of God. (2.) "*And obey his voice.*" This is the great command that is solemnly given and so often reiterated in the law with reference to God himself. (3.)

"*Do not provoke him*" or "*Do not rebel against him.*" This is the usual word whereby God expresses the transgression of his covenant—a rebellion that can be committed only against God. (4.) The reason for these commands is twofold. The first is taken from the sovereign authority of this Angel. "*For he will not pardon your transgressions.*" That is, as Joshua afterwards tells the same people, "*He is a holy God; he is a jealous God; he will not forgive your transgressions nor your sins*" (Josh 24:19)—namely, sins of rebellion that break and annul his covenant. "*Who can forgive sins but God?*" To suppose here a created angel is to open a door to gross idolatry; for the one who has absolute power to pardon and punish sin, this one may certainly be worshipped with religious adoration.

The second reason is taken from his name: "*For my name is in him.*" This is "*a more excellent name*" (Heb 1:4) than any of the angels enjoy. He is God, Jehovah, that is his name; and he answers to it. Hence, Exodus 23:22 adds, "*If you will truly obey his voice and do all that I say…*" His voice is the voice of God, and when he speaks God speaks. Thus, the people's obedience depends on the accomplishment of the promise. Moreover, in Exodus 33:14, God says concerning this Angel, "*My presence* ("*my face*"; *panim*) *shall go with you.*" Moses calls this presence the "glory" (18). This essential glory was manifested to him (34:6), though it was obscure in comparison to what was shown to them who, in his human nature said, *"In him the whole fullness of deity dwells bodily"* (Col 2:9) and *"we have seen his glory, glory as of the only Son from the Father"* (John 1:14).

This face of God is the face of the one of whom it says, *"Whoever has seen me has seen the Father"* (John 14:9). This is because he is *"the radiance of the glory of God and the exact imprint of his nature"* (Heb 1:3). He accompanied the people in the wilderness (1Co 10:4). Moses prayed for his merciful good pleasure towards them (Dt 33:16)—that is, *"Every good gift and every perfect gift that comes down from the Father of lights"* (Jam 1:17). These things evidently express God, and no one else; and yet he is said to be an angel sent of God, in his name, and to his work. Thus, he can be none other than a certain person of the Godhead who accepted the task and was thus revealed to the church, as the one who was to take upon him the seed of Abraham, in order to be their eternal Redeemer.

18. Josh 5:13–15, *"When Joshua was by Jericho, he lifted up his eyes and looked, and behold, a man was standing before him with his drawn sword in his hand. And Joshua went to him and said to him, 'Are you for us, or for our adversaries?' And he said, 'No; but I am the commander of the army of the LORD. Now I have come.' And Joshua fell on his face to the earth and worshiped and said to him, 'What does my lord say to his servant?' And the commander of the LORD's army said to Joshua, 'Take off your sandals from*

your feet, for the place where you are standing is holy.' And Joshua did so."

The appearance here is of a man, *"a man of war"* (13), just as God is called in Exodus 15:3, armed, with his sword drawn in his hand, as a sign of the business he came to do. At first sight, Joshua apprehends him to be only a man; which prompted his question, *"Are you for us, or for our adversaries?"* This question displays his courage and undaunted magnanimity; for doubtless the appearance was imposing and glorious. But he answers his question *lo*, "I am not." That is, a man neither of your party nor of his enemy's, but quite another person, *"the Prince of the LORD's host."* And this was another renowned manifestation of the Son of God to the church of old, accompanied with many instructive circumstances.

1. From the *shape* in which he appeared, namely, that of a man, as a pledge of his future incarnation.
2. From the *title* that he assumes to himself, *"The Captain of the LORD's host,"* he to whom the guidance and conduct of them towards sabbath rest, not only temporal but eternal, was committed. Hence the apostle, in allusion to this place and title, calls him *"The Captain of our salvation"* (Heb 2:10).
3. The *person* to whom he spoke when he gave himself this title was the captain of the people at that time; teaching both him and them that

there was another, supreme Captain of their eternal deliverance.

4. From the *time and place* of his appearance, which was upon the entrance of he and his family into Canaan, and the first opposition which he immediately met with Esau. Thus, he engages his presence with his church in all things which oppose them in their way to eternal rest.

5. From the *adoration and worship* which Joshua gave to him; which he accepted, contrary to the duty and practice of created angels (Rev 19:10; 22:8, 9).

6. From the *prescription of the ceremonies* expressing religious reverence, "*Take off your shoes;*" with the reason added, "*For the place where you stand 'is holy,*" made so by, of course, by the presence of God; the same command that was given to Moses by the God of Abraham, Isaac, and Jacob (Ex 3:5).

By all these things the church was instructed in the person, nature, and office of the Son of God, even in the mystery of his eternal distinct subsistence in the Godhead, his future incarnation and condescension to the office of being the Head and Savior of his church.

19. These manifestations of the Son of God to the church of old, as the Angel or Messenger of the Father, existing in his own divine person, are each of them *revelations* of the promised Seed, the great and

only Savior and Deliverer of the church, in his eternal pre-existence prior to his incarnation; and *pledges* of his future taking our flesh for the accomplishment of all the word committed to him by the Father. Many other instances of this similar nature could be added from the early and later prophets; which, because in the most important circumstances they are coextensive with these, but we do not need to talk about them here.

20. Some late interpreters would apply all these appearances to a created delegated angel. The conceit of this is irreconcilable with the sacred text, as we have already shown, and it is contrary to the sense of the ancient writers of the Christian church. A large collection of testimonies from them is not suited to our present design and purpose. I shall therefore only mention two of the most ancient of them, one of the Latin Fathers, the other of the Greek.

The first is Tertullian, who tells us, "*Christ always dealt (with men) in the name of God the Father; and so he himself conversed with the patriarchs and prophets from the very beginning*" (*Against Marcion, lib.* ii). And again, "*It was Christ who descended into communion with men, from Adam to the patriarchs and prophets, in visions, dreams, and appearances, or representations of himself, instructing them in his future condition from the beginning; and God who conversed with men on earth was no other but the Word who was to be made flesh*" (*Against Praxeas*). The other is Justin

Martyr, whose words need not be produced, seeing it is known how he contends for this very thing in his *Dialogue with Trypho*.

21. That which is more direct to our purpose is to inquire into the apprehensions of the Jewish masters concerning the *divine appearances* that were given to the patriarchs and church of old, with what may thus be collected for their conviction concerning the person of the Messiah. Most of their expositors do, I confess, pass over the difficulties of the places mentioned (I mean those which need to further their present infidelity) without taking the least notice of them. Some would have the angel mentioned to be Michael, to whom they assign a privilege above all the other angels, angels who preside over other countries. But who that Michael is, and what that privilege consists of, they do not know. Some say that Michael is the high priest of heaven, who offers up the prayers of the righteous. So R. Menachem. *"He is the priest above, who offers or presents the souls of the righteous,"* says another, more agreeably to the truth than they are even aware.

One chief example of this, in the words of Moses Nachmanides Gerundensis,[11] on Exodus 23, which has

---

[11] Moses ben Nahman (1194-1270), was commonly called Nachmanides or Ramban. He was a leading medieval Jewish scholar, rabbi, philosopher, physician, kabbalist, and biblical commentator who lived in Spain but was an important figure in the reestablishment of the Jewish community in Jerusalem after the crusaders destroyed it in 1099.

been taken notice of by many, shall suffice. His words are, "This Angel, if we speak exactly, is the Angel Redeemer, concerning whom it is written, '*My name is in him*' (Ex 23:21); that Angel who said to Jacob, '*I am the God of Bethel*' (Gen 31:13); he of whom it is said, '*And God called unto Moses out of the bush*' (Ex 3:4). And he is called an Angel because he governs the world: for it is written (Dt 6:21), '*The LORD brought us out of Egypt;*' and elsewhere (Num 20:16), '*He sent his Angel, and brought us out of Egypt.*' Moreover, it is written (Isa 63:9), '*And the Angel of his face (presence) saved them,*'— namely, that Angel who is the face of God; of whom it is said (Ex 33:14), '*My face shall go before you, and I will cause you to rest.*' Lastly, it is that Angel of whom the prophet speaks (Mal 3:1), '*And the Lord, whom you seek, shall suddenly come to his temple, the Angel of the covenant, in whom you delight.*'" His following words are to the same purpose: "Mark diligently what the meaning is of these words, '*My face shall go before you;*' for Moses and the Israelites always desired the chief Angel, but who that was they could not truly understand, for neither could they learn it of any others nor obtain it by prophecy. But the '*face of God*' signifies God himself, as all interpreters acknowledge. But no man can have the least knowledge of this unless he is skilled in the mysteries of the law." He adds moreover: "'*My face shall go before you,*' that is, '*the Angel of the covenant, whom you desire, in whom my face shall be seen;*' of whom it is said, '*In an acceptable time have I heard you; my name is in him; I will cause you to rest, or cause that he shall be gentle or kind to you, nor shall lead you with rigor, but quietly and mercifully.*'"

22. R. Moses Bar Nachman wrote around the year of the Lord 1220, in Spain, and died at Jerusalem in 1260, and he is one of the chief masters of the Jews. There are many things occurring in his writings that are beyond the common present understanding of the Jews. We see this especially in the places cited where he plainly exposes one of the principal foundations of their present infidelity. For he not only grants, but contends and proves, that the Angel spoken of was God; and being sent of God as his angel, he must be a *distinct person* in the Godhead, just as we have proved.

The reason why he says he is called an Angel is, "*because he governs the world.*" Although the thing in itself is true, it is not so proper. He is called this because of his eternal designation and actual delegation by the Father to the work of saving the church, in all conditions from first to last. As he acknowledged that his being called "*The face of God*" proves him to be God, it also no less evidently reveals his personal distinction from him whose face he is—that is, "*the brightness of his glory, and the express image of his person.*" The language he adds about the mercy and kindliness of God which comes by the appointment of God, is implemented towards his people, and is a fitting symbol of the tenderness and mercy which the great Captain of our salvation exercises by God's appointment towards all those whom he leads and brings to glory.

23. It is also beneficial to consider what some of them write in *Tanchuma*, an ancient comment on the five books of Moses. Speaking of the Angel that went before them from Exodus 23:20, "God," they say, "said to Moses, *'Behold, I send my Angel before your face.'* But Moses answered, *'I will not have an angel, I will only have yourself.'* But when Joshua the son of Nun first saw the angel, he said, *'Are you for us, or for our adversaries?'* Then the angel answered, *'I am the Captain of the* LORD'S *host, and now I come.'* As if he had said, 'I have come a second time, that I may lead the Israelites into their possession. I came when Moses your master was the ruler; but when he saw me, he would not have me to go with him, but refused me.' As soon as Joshua heard this, he fell on his face and worshipped, saying, *'What does my Lord say to his servant?'*"

An answer to this in the Talmud[12] comes from a gloss on these words, *"He will not pardon your transgressions"* (Ex 23:21). It says, *"'He cannot spare or pardon your transgressions;'* what then does he do, or could he do? Thus, he said to him (to God), 'We believe that he cannot pardon our transgressions, and therefore we refuse him, and will not accept him; certainly not as a leader to go in and out before us.'" They greatly

---

[12] *Tractat. Sanhed.*, cap. iv., Echad dine Mamonoth.

mistake in supposing that the angel who Moses refused was the same who afterwards appeared to
Joshua; for the angel appearing to Joshua was the same
with him in whom was the "name of God," and who
was promised to them under the name of the face or
presence of God. But they were right enough on one
thing, not that Moses, but their *church* under the law
refused the "Angel of God's presence," who was to
conduct all who obey him into everlasting rest. And
the church of believers under Joshua, which was a
type of the church of the New Testament, when they
conformed themselves to him, found rest for their
souls.

24. This Angel of whom we have spoken is the
one whom the Talmudists call "Metatron." Ben Uzziel,[13] in his Targum on Genesis 5, ascribes this name
to Enoch. He ascended, he says, into heaven, by the
word of the Lord, "and his name was called Metatron,
the great scribe." But this opinion is rejected and con-
futed in the Talmud. There they tell us that "Metatron" is "the prince of the world," or, as Elijah calls
him in Tishbi,[14] "the prince of God's presence." The
mention of this name is in Talmud,[15] where they
plainly intimate that they meant an uncreated Angel
by this name. For they assign such things to him as are

---

[13] This is Targum Pseudo-Jonathan.
[14] Elijah Levita (1469-1549). *Tishbi* refers to his dictionary of the
Talmud, Midrash, and Targums.
[15] *Tract. Sanhed.*, cap. iv.

impossible to any other. And, as Reuchlin informs us from the Cabbalists, they say, "Metatron was the master or teacher of Moses himself." "He it is," says Elijah, "who is the angel always appearing in the presence of God; of whom it is said, 'My name is in him.'" The Talmudists add, that he has power to blot out the sins of Israel, which is why they call him "The chancellor of heaven." Bechai, a famous master among them, affirms that his name signifies both a lord, a messenger, and a keeper (on Exodus 23). A *lord*, because he rules all; a *messenger*, because he always stands before God, to do his will; and a *keeper*, because he keeps Israel.

The etymology, I confess, which he gives for this name is weak and foolish; nor is the one Elijah gives any better, when he tells us that "Metatron" is the "one sent." But it is evident that what they intend by these obscure guesses, which are the corrupted relics of ancient traditions, namely, the uncreated Prince of glory, who, being Lord of all, appeared long ago to the patriarchs as the angel or messenger of the Father. As for the word itself, it is either a corrupt expression of the Latin "mediator," such as is usual amongst them, or a made-up word using gematria in order to answer to *Shaddai*, the "Almighty," given that there is numerical significance to their letters.[16]

---

[16] *Metatron.* No one to this day quite knows the origin of this name. Sometimes called "lesser Yahweh," some have suggested the possibility that the "him" in Ex 23:21 ("because my name is within him

This was another way in which God instructed the church of old in the mystery of the person of the Messiah who was promised to them.[17]

[the Angel])" refers to Metatron, where the *ttr* in the word comes from *tetra*, the word for "four" in Greek, and a shorthand for the Tetragrammaton—YHWH. See Andrei A. Orlov, *The Etymology of the Name 'Metatron,"* in *The Enoch-Metatron Tradition* (TSAJ, 107; Tuebiingen: Mohr-Sieback, 2005). An excerpt is here (http://www.marquette.edu/maqom/meta-tronname.html#_ftnref24).

[17] You can read the Banner of Truth version of this work in John Owen, *An Exposition of the Epistle to the Hebrews*, ed. W. H. Goold, vol. 18, Works of John Owen (Edinburgh: Johnstone and Hunter, 1854), 215–233.

The Angel in the Church Fathers

A List of Church Fathers Who See the Angel as Christ

Shepherd of Hermes (first-second century)
Similitude 7.5, 8.1.2, 8.1.5.[18]

Justin Martyr (100-165)
Dialogue with Trypho, 56.1, 58.3, 59.1, 60, 61, 62, 76, 86, 116, 126, 127, 128.

Theophilus of Antioch (late second century)
To Autolycus 2.22.

Melito (d. 190)
New Fragments, 15.

Irenaeus (135-202)
Against Heresies, 3.6.1-5 ; 4.10.1.

---

[18] The Shepherd is the oldest of our non-biblical documents. It is saturated with angel language and other terms (Shepherd, The Angel of Repentance, The Angel of Punishment, The Most Revered Angel, The Glorious Angel, etc.) that are clearly Christological at times. But it is an apocalyptic book with difficult symbols and its exact understanding of the Angel of the LORD and Christ can be difficult to nail down. Here are a couple of places to start: Charles A. Gieschen, *Angelomorphic Christology: Antecedents & Early Evidence* (Boston: Brill, 1998), 214-28; Bogdan G. Bucur, "The Son of God and the Angelomorphic Holy Spirit: A Rereading of the Shepherd's Christology," *ZNW* 98 (2007): 120-42.

Fragments, 53.
Proof of Apostolic Preaching (44-46).
Clement of Alexandria (150-215)
The Instructor, 1.7.
Tertullian (155-225)
Against Praxeas, 16.
De Carne, 14.
Against Marcion 2.27, 3.9.6.
Origen (185-254)
Against Celsus, 5.53, 8.27.
> *(in Jerome Ep 71 ad Vigilant "He is wrong about the resurrection of the body, he is wrong about the condition of souls and the repentance of the devil, and more grave than all this, he testifies that the Son and the Holy Spirit are Seraphim.")*
Hippolytus (fl. 222-245)
Fragments from Commentaries, On Daniel Frag. 25.
Apostolic Tradition 4.4.
Cyprian (200-258)
Against the Jews 2.5.
Novatian (fl. 235-258)
On the Trinity, 18, 19, 31.
Apostolic Constitutions, 5.3.20.
Letter of the Six Bishops[19] to Paul of Samosata (aka Letter of Hymenaeus)
Methodius (d. 311)
Symposium, 3.4.
Lactantius (260-330)
The Divine Institutes 4.6.1.
Constantine (d. 337)
Eusebius, *Life of Constantine* 3.52.3.
Eusebius (260-340)

---

[19] Hymenaeus, Theophilus, Theotecnus, Maximus, Proclus, and Bolanus. Full Latin and Greek text (Mansi, *Sacrorum Conciliorum Nova et Amplissima Collectio*, Vol. I, pp. 1033-40): https://babel.hathitrust.org/cgi/pt?id=njp.32101078252002;view=1up;seq=557

The Proof of the Gospel, 1.5, 4.10, 5.10.
Church History, 1.2.7-8.
Preparation for the Gospel, VII. 5, 14-15.
Pseudo-Clementine (third-fourth century)
Rec 1.52.
Hilary of Poitiers (315-367)
On the Trinity 4.25.
Athanasius (325-373)
Against the Arians, 1.38, 2.13, 3.25.12-14.
Cyril of Jerusalem. (313-386)
Catechetical Lectures 12.16.
Gregory of Elvira (fl. 359-85)
On Faith 80.
Tractates on the Books of Holy Scripture 2.10-11.
Basil the Great (329-379)
Against Eunomius 2.18.
Ambrose (330-397)
Exposition of the Christian Faith, 1.13.83.
Gregory of Nyssa (335-394)
Against Eunomius, 11.3.
Council of Sirmium (351).
Chromatius of Aqueilea (fl. 400)
Sermon on the Washing of the Feet 15.2-3.
Chrysostom (344-407)
Homily on Gen 41.3, 42.2, *Theatr.* 3.
Augustine (354-430)
Jerome (347-420)
Commentary on Daniel 8:15.
Apostolic Constitutions (381-394)
5.20.
Theodoret of Cyrus (393-466)
Questions on the Octateuch Q. 90 on Genesis.
Questions on the Octateuch Q. 5 On Exodus.
Sozomen (Salminius Hermias Sozomenus) (400-450)
Church Histories 2.4.2-3.
Fulgentius (467-532)

To Monimus, 2.3.3.
Pseudo-Dionysius the Areopagite (5th-6th century)
Corpus Areopagiticum 7-9; *Epistle* 9.1 (1105A)

The Angel According to the Fathers

Adam in the Garden

The God and Father, indeed, cannot be contained, and is not found in a place, for there is no place of His rest; but His Word, through whom He made all things, being His Power and His Wisdom, assuming the role of the Father and Lord of all, went to the garden and conversed with Adam [...]. John says, "*In the beginning was the Word, and the Word was with God*" (John 1:1), showing that at first God was alone, and the Word was in Him. Then he says, "*The Word was God; all things came into existence through Him; and apart from Him not one thing came into existence*" (John 1:1-2). The Word, then, being God, and being naturally produced from God, whenever the Father of the universe wills, He sends Him to any place; and He, coming, is both heard and seen, being sent by Him, and is found in a place.

(Theophilus of Antioch, *To Autolycus* 2.22)

And first, in that which is written in Genesis, *viz.*, that God spoke with man whom He had formed out of the dust; if we set apart the figurative meaning, and treat it so as to place faith in the narrative even in the letter, it should appear that God then spoke with man in the appearance of a man ... For I do not see how such a walking and conversation of God can be understood literally, except He appeared as a man ... Who then was He? Whether the Father, or the Son, or the Holy Spirit? [Augustine seems to think the best option is that it is the Father, but adds] ... possibly, it might be that the Scripture passed over in a hidden way from person to person, and while it had related that the Father said, "*Let there be light*," and the rest which it mentioned Him to have done by the Word, went on to indicate the Son as speaking to the first man.

(Augustine, *On the Trinity* 2.10)[20]

---

[20] I put Augustine here to let his words speak for themselves. However, it needs to be pointed out that Augustine really changed the discussion on theophanies, inserting into the tradition a "revolutionary proposal" (Bogdan G. Bucur, "Scholarship on the Old Testament Roots of Trinitarian Theology: Blind Spots and Blurred Vision," in *The Bible and Early Trinitarian Theology*, ed. Christopher A. Beely and Mark E. Weedman [Washington, D. C.: The Catholic University of America Press, 2018]: 36-37). What was the proposal? We mentioned it earlier. Essentially, a created angel was "used" by the *Logos*, but was not the *Logos*. "Theophanies may (1) take the form of an angel, or (2) angels may change material bodies to facilitate the theophany, or (3) theophanies may involve a purpose-made body that is discarded after use (like the Burning Bush or the Pillar of Fire). Exodus 3:6 involved, Augustine considered, a real created angel. God's presence, however, was really only in him inasmuch as the Angel speaks *ex persona Dei* (III.10.20) (but on the other hand, it may be said the Word of God was in the angelic manifestation on Sinai in the sense that he was present in the Laws and that the theophany anticipated the Incarnation). Fundamentally, the stuff of theophanies was created and then discarded, and thus different from the divine essence … So, unlike the earlier writers, who saw the angel as a reference to Christ in the form of an angel, Augustine held that the theophany involved both a real created angel and God, who spoke through him. God was not present himself but was impersonated by the angel" (Robert J. Wilkinson, *Tetragrammaton: Western Christians and the Hebrew Name of God: From the Beginnings to the Seventeenth Century* [Boston: Brill, 2015], 144). What accounts for this? "Augustine, under the pressure of the Arian controversy and fearing that such identification might lead to the Son being considered a creature, considered the angel merely to *represent* the Son and to speak in his name" (144-145). See also Bogdan G. Bucur, "Augustine on Theophanies: An Orthodox Perspective," *St. Vladimir's Theological Quarterly* 52.1 (2008): 67-93.

The LORD First Meets with Abram

[Genesis 12:1]. It is not clear whether a voice alone came to the ears of Abraham, or whether anything also appeared to his eyes. But a little while after, it is somewhat more clearly said, "And the Lord appeared unto Abraham, and said, 'Unto thy seed will I give this land'" (Gen 12:7). But neither there is it expressly said in what form God appeared to him, nor whether the Father, or the Son, or the Holy Spirit appeared to him. Unless, perhaps, they think that it was the Son who appeared to Abraham, because it is not written, God appeared to him, but "the Lord appeared to him." For the Son seems to be called the Lord as though the name was appropriated to Him; as *e.g.* the apostle says, "For though there be that are called gods, whether in heaven or in earth, (as there be gods many and lords many,) but to us there is but one God, the Father, of whom are all things, and we in Him; and one Lord Jesus Christ, by whom are all things, and we by Him."

(Augustine, *On the Trinity* 2.10)

Therefore, let it be altogether verified that they are sharers in the divine blessing and participants in the spiritual grace who, it is apparent, are followers of the faith of Abraham in sacrifice. In the book of Genesis we read: "Then the Lord appeared to Abraham and said, 'To your offspring I will give this land.' So he built there an altar to the Lord who had appeared to him. From there he moved on to the hill country on the east of Bethel and pitched his tent with Bethel on the west ... and there he built an altar to the Lord God and invoked the name of the Lord God." Now let the heretics choose what they want, that either they confess that the Father was seen by Abraham or certainly agree that the altar was built by Abraham to the Son. The reading of the Old Testament frequently indicates that the altar was built for no other reason than that sacrifice must be offered to God.

(Fulgentius, *To Monimus* 2.3.3)

The Angel and Hagar

It is the Angel of God Who speaks, and speaks of things far beyond the powers which a messenger, for that is the meaning of the word, could have. He says, *I will multiply your seed exceedingly, and it shall not be numbered for multitude.* The power of multiplying nations lies outside the ministry of an angel. Yet what says the Scripture of Him Who is called the Angel of God, yet speaks words which belong to God alone? *And she called the Name of the Lord that spoke with her, You are God, Who hast seen me.* First, He is the Angel of God; then He is the Lord, for *She called the Name of the Lord;* then, thirdly, He is God, for *You are God, Who hast seen me.* He Who is called the Angel of God is also Lord and

God. The Son of God is also, according to the prophet, the *Angel of Great Counsel.*

(Hilary of Poitiers, *On the Trinity* 4.22)

Abraham and the Three Visitors

And again Moses tells how the Son of God drew near to converse with Abraham: And God appeared unto him by the oak of Mamre in the middle of the day. And looking up with his eyes he beheld, and, lo, three men stood over against him. And he bowed himself down to the earth, and said: Lord, if indeed I have found favor in thy sight. And all that which follows he spoke with the Lord, and the Lord spoke with him. Now two of the three were angels; but one was the Son of God, with whom also Abraham spoke, pleading on behalf of the men of Sodom, that they should not perish if at least ten righteous should be found there. And, while these were speaking, the two angels entered into Sodom, and Lot received them. And then the Scripture says: And the Lord rained upon Sodom and Gomorrah brimstone and fire from the Lord out of heaven: that is to say, the Son, who spoke with Abraham, being Lord, received power to punish the men of Sodom from the Lord out of heaven, even from the Father who rules over all...

(Irenaeus, *Proof of Apostolic Preaching* 44)

Angels, after all, are not actually men by nature, but they resemble men in appearance. For example, three persons appeared as men to Abraham at the oak of Mamre (Gen 18:1), and yet they certainly were not men, for one of them was worshipped as the Lord. And so the Savior also stated in the Gospel: "Abraham beheld My day; he beheld it and rejoiced" (John 8:56).

(Jerome, Commentary on Daniel 8:15)

Abraham Sacrifices his Son

While the Father does not serve as anyone's messenger, the Son is both God and "Angel of Great Counsel." It was he who announced to us the mysteries of the Father: "All I have heard from my Father I have revealed to you." Likewise, the one who called out to Abraham is referred to as both "angel" (Gen 22:11) and "God" (Gen 22:1).

(Theodoret, On Genesis Question 5)

It is recorded that here [at Mamre] the Son of God appeared to Abraham with two angels ... then there appeared to the godly man he who in later times showed himself clearly of a virgin for the salvation of the human race.

(Sozomen, Church Histories 2.4.2-3)

Christ appeared to you, O wondrous one, flanked by two angels; and through [your] care for strangers you become a messmate to God and angels. O, blessed tent, which by condescension housed God accompanied by angels! Christ appeared to you in human form, disclosing to you the mystery of the divine advent of himself and [his] salvation."

(Chrysostom, *Against Theater* 3)

Jacob and His "Ladder"

Now, note that after reporting that an angel had appeared from above, Jacob indicated that this was none other than God himself: "I am God, who appeared to you on the way." He had seen angels ascending and descending the ladder and God set firm at the top, whom he here called both "angel" and "God": "God" as to his nature, and "angel" so we would know that it was not the Father who appeared to him but the only-begotten Son.

(Theodoret, *On Genesis* Question 90)

Jacob Wrestles a Man

No doubt the Almighty Son of GOD could have appeared for the purpose of teaching, and justifying men in exactly the same way that He appeared both to patriarchs and prophets in the semblance of flesh; for instance, when He engaged in a struggle, and entered into conversation (with Jacob), or when He refused not hospitable entertainment, and even partook of the food set before Him.

(Leo the Great, *Letter* 31.2)

Jacob Blesses Joseph

[Note: This passage (Genesis 48:15-16) is the subject of a great deal of the book *The Judgement of the Ancient Jewish Church Against The Unitarians* by the French Reformer Peter Allix. His treatment of the Angel of the LORD is so masterful that we have reproduced chapters from his book, along with a treatment of the Angel given by John Owen and a whole list of quotations from this text by the Church Fathers as a companion volume to our own book on the Angel. For more, see *The Angel of the LORD in Early Jewish, Christian, and Reformation History*, published by Waters of Creation Publishing, 2019. In order to save space, we have only provided a single quotation from Athanasius here].

None of created and natural Angels did [Jacob] join to God their Creator, nor rejecting God that fed him, did he from any Angel ask the blessing on his grandsons; but in saying, 'Who delivered me from all evil,' he showed that it was no created Angel, but the Word of God, whom he joined to the Father in his prayer, through whom, whomsoever He will, God does deliver. For knowing that He is also called the Father's 'Angel of Great Counsel,' (Isa 9:6 LXX) he said that none other than He was the Giver of blessing, and Deliverer from evil."

(Athanasius, *Against the Arians* 3.25.12)

Moses and the Burning Bush

Wherefore, as I have already stated, no other is named as God, or is called Lord, except Him who is God and Lord of all, who also said to Moses, "I AM THAT I AM. And thus shalt thou say to the children of Israel: He who is, hath sent me unto you" (Ex 3:14); and His Son Jesus Christ our Lord, who makes those that believe in His name the sons of God. And again, when the Son speaks to Moses, He says, "I am come down to deliver this people" (Ex 3:8).

(Irenaeus, *Against Heresies* 3.6.2)

"And the Angel of the Lord appeared unto him in a flame of fire, out of the midst of a bush; and he looked, and, behold, the bush burned with fire, and the bush was not consumed. And Moses said, I will now turn aside, and see this great sight, why the bush is not burnt. And when the Lord saw that he turned aside to see, God called unto him out of the midst of the bush, and said, I am the God of thy father, the God of Abraham, the God of Isaac, and the God of Jacob" (Ex 3:1-6).

He is here also first called the Angel of the Lord, and then God. Was an angel, then, the God of Abraham, and the God of Isaac, and the God of Jacob? Therefore He may be rightly understood to be the Saviour Himself, of whom the apostle says, *"Whose are the fathers, and of whom as concerning the flesh Christ came, who is over all, God blessed forever"* (Rom 9:5). He, therefore, *"who is over all, God blessed forever,"* is not unreasonably here understood also to be Himself the God of Abraham, the God of Isaac, and the God of Jacob. But why is He previously called the Angel of the Lord, when He appeared in a flame of fire out of the bush? Was it because it was one of many angels, who by an economy [or arrangement] bare the person of his Lord? or was something of the creature assumed by Him in order to bring about a visible appearance for the business in hand, and that words might thence be audibly uttered, whereby the presence of the Lord might be shown, in such way as was fitting, to the corporeal senses of man, by means of the creature made subject? For if he was one of the angels, who could easily affirm whether it was the person of the Son which was imposed upon him to announce, or that of the Holy Spirit, or that of God the Father, or altogether of the Trinity itself, who is the one and only God, in order that he might say, *"I am the God of Abraham, and the God of Isaac, and the God of Jacob?"* For we cannot say that the Son of God is the God of Abraham, and the God of Isaac, and the God of Jacob, and that the Father is not; nor will anyone dare to deny that either the Holy Spirit, or the Trinity itself, whom we believe and understand to be the one God, is the God of Abraham, and the God of Isaac, and the God of Jacob. For he who is not God, is not the God of those fathers. Furthermore, if not only the Father is God, as all, even heretics, admit; but also the Son, which, whether they will or not, they are compelled to acknowledge, since the apostle says, *"Who is over all, God blessed forever;"* and the Holy Spirit, since the same apostle says, *"Therefore glorify God in your body;"* when he had said above, *"Know ye not that your body is the temple of the Holy Ghost, which is in you, which ye have of God?"* (1Co 6:19-20), and these three are one God, as catholic soundness believes: it is not sufficiently apparent which person of the Trinity that angel bare, if he was one of the rest of the angels, and whether any person, and not rather that of the Trinity itself. But if the creature was assumed for the purpose of the business in hand, whereby both to appear to human eyes, and to sound in human ears, and to be called the Angel of the Lord, and the Lord, and God; then cannot God here be understood to be the Father, but either the Son or the Holy Spirit. Although I cannot call to mind that the Holy Spirit is anywhere else called an angel, which yet may be understood from His work; for it is said of Him, *"And He will show you things to come"* (John 16:13); and "angel" in Greek is certainly equivalent to "messenger" in Latin: but we read most evidently of the Lord Jesus Christ in the prophet, that He is called *"the Angel of Great Counsel"* (Isa 9:6), while both the Holy Spirit and the Son of God is God and Lord of the angels.

(Augustine, *On the Trinity* 2.13)[21]

I Send My Angel

And accordingly it is agreed that the Son of God Himself spoke to Moses, and said to the people, "Behold, I send mine angel before thy"—that is, the people's— "face, to guard thee on the march, and to introduce thee into the land which I have prepared thee: attend to him, and be not disobedient to him; for he hath not escaped thy notice, since my name is upon him."

(Tertullian, *Against the Jews* 9)

---

[21] Augustine wrestled with the question of whether or not the Angel is the Son. Most scholarship believes he did not think the Angel was the Son, but the few excerpts we have given in this chapter from him seem to point in the other direction. Whatever the case, the comment by William Shedd here on Augustine is certainly worth pondering. "The theophanies of the Pentateuch are trinitarian in their implication. They involve distinctions in God—God sending, and God sent; God speaking of God, and God speaking to God. The trinitarianism of the Old Testament has been lost sight of to some extent in the modern construction of the doctrine. The patristic, mediæval, and reformation theologies worked this vein with thoroughness, and the analysis of Augustin in this reference is worthy of careful study." W. G. T. Shedd, in Philip Schaff, ed., *St. Augustin: On the Holy Trinity, Doctrinal Treatises, Moral Treatises*, vol. 3, A Select Library of the Nicene and Post-Nicene Fathers of the Christian Church, First Series (Buffalo, NY: Christian Literature Company, 1887), p. 47 n. 3.

Now, as he is also called "angel" we should realize that it was not God the Father who appeared to Moses. After all, is the Father anyone's messenger? Rather, it was the only-begotten Son, 'The Angel of the Great Counsel," he who said to the sacred disciples, "All I have heard from my Father I have revealed to you." As Scripture uses the term "Angel," not to suggest a subordinate minister, but to indicate the person of the Only-begotten, so it goes on to proclaim his nature and authority when it relates that he declared "I am who am," and "I am the God of Abraham, the God of Isaac, and the God of Jacob. This is my everlasting name and memorial for all generations." This indicates his divinity and shows his everlasting eternity.

(Theodoret,
Questions on the Octateuch: On Exodus Q.5)

Joshua 5: The Commander of the Hosts

'I shall give you another testimony, my friends,' said I, 'from the Scriptures, that God begat before all creatures a Beginning, [who was] a certain rational power [proceeding] from Himself, who is called by the Holy Spirit, now the Glory of the Lord, now the Son, again Wisdom, again an Angel, then God, and then Lord and Logos; and on another occasion He calls Himself

Captain, when He appeared in human form to Joshua the son of Nave (Nun).'

(Justin Martyr, *Dialogue* 61)

Daniel 3: The Fiery Furnace

He who delivered the Young Men from the flames took flesh and came upon the earth. Nailed to the Cross, he granted us salvation, the God of our fathers, alone blessed and greatly glorified ... The Offspring of the Mother of God saved the innocent Youths in the furnace.

(Romanos the Melodist,
Canon of Holy Cross for Third Sunday in Lent, Ode 7 and
Canon of Akathist, Ode 8, Erimos)

The Angel in Revelation

[The priest] offers this prayer for Christ's mystical body, which is signified in this sacrament, that the angel standing by at the Divine mysteries may present to God the prayers of both priest and people, according to Rev 8:4: *And the smoke of the incense of the prayers of the saints ascended up before God, from the hand of the angel* ... by the angel we are to understand Christ Himself, Who is the *Angel of Great Counsel* (Isa 9:6: *LXX*), Who unites His mystical body with God the Father and the Church triumphant.

(Thomas *Summa* III q. 83, a. 4, ad 9)

Various OT Angel Appearances Together

The Son of God is implanted everywhere throughout his writings: at one time, indeed, speaking with Abraham, when about to eat with him; at another time ... bringing down judgment upon the Sodomites; and again when He becomes visible and directs Jacob on his journey, and speaks with Moses from the bush.

(Irenaeus, *Against Heresies* 4.10.1)

He who hung the earth is hanging

He who fixed the heavens in place has been fixed in place

He who laid the foundations of the universe has been laid on a tree...

Today, He who hung the earth upon the waters is hung upon the Cross...

He who in the Jordan set Adam free receives blows upon His face...

He who rained manna down on the people in the wilderness is fed on milk from His Mother's breast.

(Melito of Sardis, *On Pascha* 96; *Antiphon* 15; *Ninth Hour of the Eve of Nativity: Glory Sticheron*)

That Christ is at once Angel and God. In Genesis, to Abraham: "And the Angel of the Lord called him from heaven, and said to him, 'Abraham, Abraham!' And he said, 'Here am I.' And He said, 'Do not lay a hand upon the lad, neither do anything to him. For now I know that you fear God, and have not spared your son, your beloved son, for my sake." Also in the same place, to Jacob: "And the Angel of the Lord spoke to me in dreams, I am God, whom you saw in the place of God where you anointed a pillar of stone to me, and vowed to me a vow." Also in Exodus: "But God went before them by day indeed in a pillar of cloud, to show them the way; and by night in a pillar of fire." And afterwards, in the same place: "And the Angel of God moved forward, which went before the army of the children of Israel." Also in the same place: "Behold, I send my Angel before your face, to keep you in the way, that He may lead you into the land which I have prepared for you. Observe Him, and obey Him, and be not disobedient to Him, for He will not pardon your transgression. For my Name is in Him." As He Himself says in the Gospel: "I came in the name of my Father, and you received me not. But if another shall come in his own name, him you will receive." And again, in the 118th Psalm: "Blessed is He who cometh in the name of the Lord." Also in Malachi: "My covenant of life and peace was with Levi; and I gave him fear, that he should fear me, that he should go from the face of my name. The law of truth was in his mouth, and unrighteousness was not found in his lips. In the peace of the tongue correcting, he walked with us, and turned many away from unrighteousness. Because the lips of the priests shall keep knowledge, and they shall seek the law at His mouth; for He is the Angel of the Almighty."

(Cyprian, Against the Jews 2.5)

It is the Son who has been from the beginning administering judgment, throwing down the haughty tower, and dividing the tongues, punishing the whole world by the violence of waters, raining upon Sodom and Gomorrah fire and brimstone, as the LORD from the LORD. For He it was who at all times came down to hold converse with men, from Adam on to the patriarchs and the prophets, in vision, in dream, in mirror, in dark saying ... [He did this] in order to level for us the way of faith, that we might the more readily believe that the Son of God had come down into the world, if we knew that in times past also something similar had been done.[22]

(Tertullian, Against Praxeas 16)

---

[22] Foster writes, "Tertullian is extremely reluctant to identify Christ as an angel in the same way that Michael and Gabriel are angels. Additionally, Tertullian explicitly states that Christ is only an angel according to function and not with respect to His substance." Nevertheless, he does apply the term to Christ in his quotation of Isa 9:6 LXX, "Certainly he is described as an angel of great counsel, 'angel' meaning 'messenger', by a term of office, not of nature: for he was to announce to the world the Father's great project, concerned with the restitution of man." Edgar G. Foster, *Angelomorphic Christology and the Exegesis of Psalm 8:5 in Tertullians' Adversus Praxean: An Examination of Tertullian's Reluctance to Attribute Angelic Properties to the Son of God* (New York: University Press of America, Inc., 2005), 7.

Was it without reason that Christ was made Man? Are our teachings ingenious phrases and human subtleties? Are not the Holy Scriptures our salvation? Are not the predictions of the Prophets? Keep then, I pray thee, this deposit undisturbed, and let none remove thee: believe that God became Man. But though it has been proved possible for Him to be made Man, yet if the Jews still disbelieve, let us hold this forth to them what strange thing do we announce in saying that God was made Man, when yourselves say that Abraham received the Lord as a guest? What strange thing do we announce, when Jacob says, For I have seen God face to face, and my life is preserved? The Lord, who ate with Abraham, ate also with us.

(Cyril, *Catechetical Lectures* 12.16)

When they assemble together, they read the Lamentations of Jeremiah, in which it is said, "The Spirit before our face, Christ the Lord was taken in their destructions" (Lam 4:20 LXX); and Baruch, in whom it is written, "This is our God; no other shall be esteemed with Him. He found out every way of knowledge, and showed it to Jacob His son, and Israel His beloved. Afterwards He was seen upon earth, and conversed with men" (Baruch 3:25-37) ... To Him did Moses bear witness, and said: "The Lord received fire from the Lord, and rained it down." Him did Jacob see as a man, and said: "I have seen God face to face, and my soul is preserved." Him did Abraham entertain, and acknowledge to be the Judge, and his Lord. Him did Moses see in the bush; concerning Him did he speak in Deuteronomy: "A Prophet will the Lord your God raise up" ... Him did Joshua the son of Nun see, as the captain of the Lord's host, in armor, for their assistance against Jericho; to whom he fell down, and worshipped, as a servant does to his master. Him Samuel knew as the "Anointed of God," and thus named the priests and the kings the anointed. Him David knew, and sung an hymn concerning Him, "A song concerning the Beloved" ... Concerning Him also Solomon spoke, as in His person: "The Lord created me the beginning of His ways, for His works: before the world He founded me, in the beginning before He made the earth, before the fountains of waters came, before the mountains were fastened; He begat me before all the hills" ... Him Daniel describes as "the Son of man coming to the Father," and receiving all judgment and honor from Him ... Ezekiel also, and the following prophets, affirm everywhere that he is the Christ, the Lord, the King, the Judge, the Lawgiver, the Angel of the Father, the only-begotten God. Him therefore do we also preach to you, and declare him to be God the Word, who ministered to his God and Father for the creation of the universe.

(*Apostolic Constitutions* 5.20)

Know then that Christ, who was from the beginning, and always, was ever present with the pious, though secretly, through all their generations; especially those who waited for Him, to whom he frequently appeared.

(Pseudo-Clementines, *Rec* 1.52)

But our Instructor is the holy God Jesus, the Word, who is the guide of all humanity ... when He speaks in His own person, He confesses Himself to be the Instructor: "*I am the Lord your God, who brought thee out of the land of Egypt.*" Who, then, has the power of leading in and out? Is it not the Instructor? This was He who appeared to Abraham, and said to him, "*I am your God, be accepted before Me;*" and in a way most befitting an instructor, forms him into a faithful child, saying, "*And be blameless; and I will make My covenant between Me and you, and your seed.*" There is the communication of the Instructor's friendship. And He most manifestly appears as Jacob's instructor. He says accordingly to him, "*Behold, I am with you, to keep you in all the way in which thou shalt go; and I will bring thee back into this land: for I will not leave you till I do what I have told thee.*" He is said, too, to have wrestled with Him. "*And Jacob was left alone, and there wrestled with him a man (the Instructor) till the morning.*" This was the man who led, and brought, and wrestled with, and anointed the athlete Jacob against evil. Now that the Word was at once Jacob's trainer and the Instructor of humanity [appears from this]—"He asked," it is said, "*His name, and said to him, Tell me what is your name.*" And he said, "*Why is it that thou ask My name?*" For He reserved the new name for the new people—the babe; and was as yet unnamed, the Lord God not having yet become man. Yet Jacob called the name of the place, "*Face of God.*" "*For I have seen,*" he says, "*God face to face; and my life is preserved*" (Gen 32:30). The face of God is the Word by whom God is manifested and made known. Then also was he named Israel, because he saw God the Lord. It was God, the Word, the Instructor, who said to him again afterwards, "*Fear not to go down into Egypt.*" See how the Instructor follows the righteous man, and how He anoints the athlete, teaching him to trip up his antagonist.

It is He also who teaches Moses to act as instructor. For the Lord says, "*If any one sin before Me, him will I blot out of My book; but now, go and lead this people into the place which I told thee.*" Here He is the teacher of the art of instruction. For it was really the Lord that was the instructor of the ancient people by Moses; but He is the instructor of the new people by Himself, face to face. "*For behold,*" He says to Moses, "*My angel shall go before you,*" representing the evangelical and commanding power of the Word, but guarding the Lord's prerogative. "*In the day on which I will visit them,*" He says, "*I will bring their sins on them; that is, on the day on which I will sit as judge I will render the recompense of their sins.*" For the same who is Instructor is judge, and judges those who disobey Him; and the loving Word will not pass over their transgression in silence. He reproves, that they may repent.

(Clement of Alexandria, *The Instructor* 1.7)

Who is eager for distinction in piety in this way? Who has made as great a show of being a lover of Christ as these men have, even though they boast of their arrogant and dishonorable words that go so far as to destroy the glory of the Only-Begotten? You godless man! Please stop saying that he does not exist when he is the one who truly exists, the one who is the source of life, and the one who produces being for all that exists. Didn't he find a designation well-suited for himself and fitting for his own eternity when he named himself *He Who Is* in his oracle to Moses his servant? He said: *I am He Who Is.* No one will object when I say that these words were spoken in the person of the Lord, at least no one who does not have *the veil* of the Jews upon his heart *when he reads Moses* (2Co 3:15). It is written that the angel of the Lord appeared to Moses in the bush burning with fire. After mentioning the angel at the outset of the narrative, scripture introduces the voice of God when it says that he said to Moses: *I am the God of your father Abraham.* A little further on, the same one said: *I am He Who Is.* So, then, who is this one who is both angel and God alike? Isn't it he whom we have learned is called by the name *the Angel of Great Counsel* (Isa 9:6)?

For my part, I don't think that this needs much demonstration; just mentioning it suffices for the lovers of Christ. But the incorrigible are not going to derive any benefit from a flurry of words. Even though *the Angel of Great Counsel* comes later, it remains true that previously he did not disdain the designation 'angel.' You see, it is not only in this passage that we find the scriptures naming our Lord both 'angel' and 'God.' For when Jacob narrated an appearance to his wives, he said: *And the angel of God said to me* (Gen 31:11). And a little further on, it was said: *I am the God who appeared to you in the place where you anointed a pillar to me.* In addition, it was said to Jacob as he stood before the pillar: *I am the Lord, the God of Abraham your father and the God of Isaac* (Gen 28:13). The one who is called 'angel' in the former passage is the same as the one who said in the latter passage that he appeared to Jacob. So, then, it is clear to all that, where the same one is designated both 'angel' and 'God,' it is the Only-Begotten who is revealed, manifesting himself to human beings from generation to generation and announcing the will of the Father to his saints. Consequently, when he named himself *He Who Is* before Moses, he is understood to be none other than God the Word, who *was in the beginning with God* (John 1:2).

(Basil, *Against Eumonius* 2.18)

The Angel in the Reformation

Note: I have updated the language and punctuation from many of these earlier titles for ease of reading.

Adam in the Garden

It is generally agreed among Divines, that Adam in the State of Perfection knew God in Trinity and Unity … Jerome Zanchi thinks it very injurious to Adam, to believe that he had not as great favor shown him before the Fall, as Abraham, Moses, and others had since the Fall; and thereupon asserts, that Adam being then to be sure the beloved of God, Jehovah the Son exhibited himself visibly to him, and talked with him, and made himself known to him, as his God and Governor, before he gave him the precepts of obedience, as he did to the Jews, before he gave the law to Moses. And he tells us, that several of the ancients, Justin, Irenaeus, Tertullian, [Epiphanius], and many more, were of that mind, that it was Jehovah the Son who created Adam, placed him in Paradise, appeared visibly to him, discoursed with him, and whose voice he heard, and at which he trembled when he had transgressed.

Jerome Zanchi (1516-1590)[23]

Noah and Babel

When Jehovah saw the earth, it was corrupt; for all flesh had corrupted its way upon the earth. And this wickedness became so great ... in the days of Noah; it repented Jehovah that he had made man; and it grieved him to the heart. So, after having given warning by his preacher of righteousness for 120 years, till eight persons only were left uncorrupted, he destroyed that obstinate and impenitent generation; just time enough to save one family ... And from the Mosaic account of this Jehovah, that the sins of mankind grieved him to the heart, agreeable to what is said of him in other parts of Scripture; and from his making a covenant with Noah, we have reason to conclude; that it was not the Supreme Jehovah in Person, but the Angel of the Covenant.

---

[23] Zanchi, *de creat.* 1.I.c.i.§12. As discussed in Gerard De Gols, *A Vindication of the Worship of the Lord Jesus Christ as the Supreme God, in all the Dispensations, Patriarchal, Mosaic, and Christian Demonstrating that Christ was So Known and Worshiped in all Ages, from Adam to this Day* (London: J. Darby and T. Browne, 1726), 115-116. This book is a diamond in the rough and recommended as one of the more comprehensive treatments of our subject. We have republished a portion of it in this series.

After this all men lived together in Chaldea ... Jehovah (that is, Christ, the Jehovah Angel) came down to see the city and Tower (Gen 11:4), which the children of men built; and, in order to restrain them from their undertaking, he confounded their language; and scattered them abroad upon the face of all the earth.

Henry Taylor (1711-1785)[24]

Hagar

That God might make evident the exceeding care he had of them, he sent an Angel to Hagar, and willed her to return unto her Master: which Angel, some think was the Son of God, for he was called by the name of Jehovah (Gen 16) which name was not communicated to any created Angel.

Heinrich Bünting (1545-1606)[25]

Abraham

When Abraham believed ... God is so well-pleased with his faith, that he swears ... *"I will bless you, and I*

---

[24] Henry Taylor, *The Apology of Benjamin Ben Mordecai To His Friends, for Embracing Christianity* (London: J. Wilkie, 1771), 59-60. Taylor was not entirely orthodox, but you can find the same general idea in people like De Gols, 105.

25 Heinrich Bünting, *Itinerarium totius Sacræ Scripturæ, or, The Travels of the Holy Patriarchs, Prophets, Judges, Kings, our Saviour Christ and his Apostles* ... Collected Out of the Works of Henry Bunting; and done into English by R.B. (London, J. Harefinch for T. Basset, 1682), 67. Because Bünting only alludes to his view here, we have offered another quotation from him a little later.

will multiply your seed as the stars of the heaven, and as the sand which is upon the sea-shore" (Gen 22:17). And the angel of the Lord, (viz. the Lord Jesus, as his own words show, vs. 12, 15, 16.) calls unto Abraham out of heaven and shows his admirable love in providing a ram for a burnt-offering. Thus, in believing times, the Lord reveals his love to his people.

Thomas Brooks (1608-1680)[26]

Jacob's Ladder

Whosoever is assured of this Ladder (that reaches from Heaven to Earth) may well say with *Jacob,* 'Surely the Lord Jesus Christ is in this place;' here is nothing but the House of God, and here is the Gate of Heaven; as Christ himself testifies in the tenth of John, *I am the door, and whosoever enters not by me, &c.* So that Christ is the Head of his Church, the Ladder that ascends into Heaven, and the door whereby we may enter into eternal Life.

Heinrich Bünting (1545-1606)[27]

---

[26] Thomas Brooks, *A Treatise on Assurance, A New Edition Considerably Amended and Abridged* (London: J. Mathews, and J. Buckland 1778), 69-70.
[27] Bünting, 73.

Jacob Blesses Joseph: Gen 48:15-16

The Angel which redeemed me ... Many of the ancient Fathers understand this as an uncreated Angel, viz. the Second Person of the blessed Trinity. "*But the Discourse is not concerning the sending of the Son of God, in our Flesh to redeem Mankind ... and I do not know whether it be safe to call him an Angel, i.e. a Minister, or Messenger, lest we detract from his Divinity. For in conferring Blessings, he is not a Messenger or Minister, but a principle Cause together with the Father.*" These are the words of that famous Divine Georg. Calixtus, who follows St. Chrysostom, who takes this angel to be one properly so called: And thus proves the heavenly Ministers take care of Pious People. And so does St. Basil in no less than three places of his Works: Which show it was his settled opinion. But it did not enter into their thoughts that Jacob here might have the angelic protection, by the special Favor of God to them. For it is just such an expression as that of David, to a contrary purpose (Ps 35:6).

Simon Patrick (1626-1707)[28]

The Burning Bush: Exodus 3

And the Angel of the Lord appeared to him ... For thus we must believe that God, as often as he appeared of old

---

[28] Simon Patrick, *A Commentary upon the First Book of Moses, Called Genesis* (London: Chitwell, 1689), 596-97.

to the holy patriarchs, descended in some way from his majesty, that he might reveal himself as far as was useful, and as far as their comprehension would admit ... But let us inquire who this Angel was, since soon afterwards he not only calls himself Jehovah, but claims the glory of the eternal and only God. Now, although this is an allowable manner of speaking, because the angels transfer to themselves the person and titles of God ... the ancient teachers of the Church have rightly understood that the Eternal Son of God is so called in respect to his office as Mediator, which he figuratively bore from the beginning, although he really took it upon him only at his Incarnation. And Paul sufficiently expounds this mystery to us, when he plainly asserts that Christ was the leader of his people in the Desert (1Co 10:4).[29]

John Calvin (1509-1564)

To this Angel is given the essential name of God: Jehovah. Therefore, it is certain that he also was God, even our Savior Christ, by whom and through whom the Lord communicates himself unto men, who otherwise could never have any access unto such Majesty. And he is called an Angel, because he was to be sent to

---

[29] Calvin, *Harmony of the Four Last Books of Moses*, Exod. 3:2 in loc. (CTS Harmony, I, pp. 60–61). Cited in Richard A. Muller, *Post-Reformation Reformed Dogmatics: The Rise and Development of Reformed Orthodoxy; Volume 4: The Triunity of God* (Grand Rapids, MI: Baker Academic, 2003), 291–292.

be our Deliverer, whereof this Deliverance of the Jews out of Egypt was some shadow and figure. Theodoret is of the same mind, whose words are these [in Latin] ... The whole place, he says, shows it was God: but he is called an Angel, that we might know, that he which was seen, was not God the Father (for whose Angel should the Father be) but the only begotten Son of God, which is the Angel of the great Council, which said to his holy Apostles; *All things which I have heard of my Father, I have declared unto you.* And even as he gave him the name of an Angel, not meaning thereby to note any other Minister or Messenger, but to show the person of the only begotten Son: so again he sets forth both his nature & power, saying he said: I AM THAT I AM, and I the God of Abraham, the God of Isaac, the God of Jacob, etc. Hillarie also speaks to this effect in his book on the Trinity.

Gervase Babington (1550-1610)[30]

Gideon

That Gideon worshipped Christ as God, is so plain, that anyone that reads Judges the 6th chapter must believe it, or must believe that Gideon was an idolater; for as vs. 12 we find that *"the Angel of the Lord appeared*

---

[30] Gervase Babington (1550-1610), *The Workes of the Right Reverend Father in God Gervase Babington, late Bishop of Worcester. Containing Comfortable Notes Upon the Five Bookes of Moses* (London, George Eld, 1615), 214-15.

to him, and said to him, 'The Lord is with you, you mighty man of valor.'" And it appears in vs. 13 that Gideon thought it was a created angel; but vs. 14 the Lord, the Jehovah, looked upon him, convinced him that he was not a created Angel, and commissioned him to be a judge and a deliverer of Israel. Here we have still the same person speaking first as an Angel, now as the Jehovah, and assuring him of his Presence, "*I will be with you,*" in the same manner as he had done to the Patriarchs before; and when Gideon had asked for a token of his Presence, and the Angel had wrought a miracle, and then departed from him, Gideon said, "*Alas, O Lord God!*" which was not an exclamation through fear or surprise, but was a recognition of his Divinity, and an act of Adoration paid to the divine Majesty.

Gerard De Gols (d. 1737)[31]

Samson's Birth: Judges 13

The glad tidings brought to his mother, that she should have a son. The messenger was an *angel of the Lord* (v. 3), yet appearing as a man, with the aspect and garb of a prophet, or man of God. And this angel (as the learned bishop Patrick supposes, on v. 18) was the

---

Lord himself, that is, the *Word of the Lord*, who was to be the Messiah, for his name is called *Wonderful*.

Matthew Henry (1662-1714)[32]

And the angel of the LORD said to him, Why do you ask my name, seeing it *is* secret? Or, *hidden* from mortal men; or, *wonderful*, such as you cannot comprehend; my nature or essence (which is often signified by *name* in Scripture) is incomprehensible. This shows that this was the Angel of the covenant, the Son of God.

Matthew Poole (1624-1679)[33]

General Comments

Where the Person [in an OT passage] does not clearly identify itself by speaking and apparently only one Person is involved, you may follow the rule given above and be assured that you are not going wrong when you interpret the name Jehovah to refer to our Lord Jesus Christ, God's Son.

Martin Luther (1483 – 1546)[34]

---

[32] Matthew Henry, *Matthew Henry's Commentary on the Whole Bible: Complete and Unabridged in One Volume* (Peabody: Hendrickson, 1994), 356.

[33] Matthew Poole, *Annotations upon the Holy Bible*, vol. 1 (New York: Robert Carter and Brothers, 1853), 488.

[34] Martin Luther, *Luther's Works, Vol. 15: Ecclesiastes, Song of Solomon, Last Words of David, 2 Samuel 23:1-7*, ed. Jaroslav Jan Pelikan, Hilton C. Oswald, and Helmut T. Lehmann, vol. 15 (Saint Louis: Concordia Publishing House, 1999), 336. While Luther's

Moreover, their inclination to think that in various of those *Apparitions of Angels* to the ancient *Patriarchs,* it was *Christ* himself that appeared, would further have enticed them to retain this Doctrine of Preexistence of Souls, that that opinion of Christ's appearing then might be more entire and determinate; as it would be also in those that hold *Melchizedek* that blessed *Abraham* to have been *Christ:* which opinion *Cunaeus* looks upon as true; nor can *Calvin* look upon it as *strange,* if he does but hold to his own words in his readings upon *Daniel* ... And that the *Angel* that led the Israelites into the land of *Canaan* was *Christ,* seems plainly asserted 1Co 10:9. *Neither let us tempt Christ, as some of them tempted him, and perished by Serpents.* But Christ is a complexion of the Human nature with the Divine. Consider also Heb 11:26 which seems to imply that the Soul of the *Messiah* was a Patron and Protector of the *Holy seed* betimes, and had a special relation to the *Jews* above any other Nation. And therefore when he came into the world (i.e. was born, brought up and conversed among the Jews), he might the more

---

quotation occurs in the middle of a barrage of OT passages, some of which he argues proves his point here, Gieshen explains, "Luther did not invent this understanding; it is found in the New Testament. There are Old Testament texts where YHWH is speaking that are applied to the Son by New Testament writers." For example, he cites Isa 45:23-24 cited in Php 2:10-11 and Rom 14:11 or Jer 9:24 cited in 1Co 1:31 and 2Co 10:17 or Zech 12:10 cited in John 19:37. Charles A. Gieschen, "The Real Presence of the Son Before Christ: Revisiting an Old Approach to Old Testament Christology," *Concordia Theological Quarterly* 68:2 (April 2004): 124-25.

properly be said to come to *his own,* though his own knew him not (Jn 1:11).

Henry More (1614-1687)[35]

Q. 20. How was the will of God made known to the church, before it was committed to writing?

A. By immediate revelations, Gen 2:16, 17, and 3:15; by frequent appearances of the Son of God, delighting, beforehand, to try on the human likeness, Gen 18:2, compared with vs. 3, Jdg 13:11, compared with verses 18, 19; by the ministry of the holy angels, Gen 19:1, 15; Heb 2:2, and of the patriarchs, Jude, vs. 14, 15; Heb 11:7.

Ebenezer Erskine (1680-1754)[36]

It is observable, that when Christ appeared to manage the affairs of his church in this period, he often appeared in the form of that nature which he took upon him in his incarnation. So he seems to have appeared repeatedly to Moses, and particularly at that time when God spoke to him face to face, as a man speaks to his friend, and he beheld the similitude of the Lord (Num 12:8), after he had besought him to show him

---

[35] Henry More, *An explanation of the grand mystery of godliness, or, A true and faithfull representation of the everlasting Gospel of our Lord and Saviour Jesus Christ, the only begotten Son of God and sovereign over men and angels* (London, J. Flesher for W. Morden, 1660), 22-23.

[36] Ebenezer Erskine and James Fisher, *The Assembly's Shorter Catechism Explained By Way of Question and Answer* (Edinburgh: John Gray and Gavin Alston: MDCCLXV). Q. 2.20.

his glory; which was the most remarkable vision that ever he had of Christ. There was a twofold discovery that Moses had of Christ: one was spiritual, … another was external; which was that which Moses saw, when Christ passed by, and put him in a cleft of the rock. What he saw was doubtless a glorious human form, in which Christ appeared to him, and in all likelihood the form of his glorified human nature, in which he should afterwards appear. He saw not his face; for it is not to be supposed that any man could subsist under a sight of the glory of Christ's human nature as it now appears.

So it was a human form in which Christ appeared to the seventy elders, of which we have an account (Ex 24:9, 11). "*Then Moses and Aaron went up, Nadab and Abihu, and seventy of the elders of Israel. And they saw the God of Israel: and there was under his feet, as it were a paved work of sapphire-stone, and as it were the body of heaven in his clearness. And upon the nobles of the children of Israel he did not lay his hand: also they saw God, and ate and drank.*" So Christ appeared afterwards to Joshua in the form of the human nature (Josh 5:13, 14). "*And it came to pass when Joshua was by Jericho, he lift up his eyes, and looked, and behold, there stood a man over against him, with his sword drawn in his hand: and Joshua went to him, and said to him, 'Are you for us, or for our adversaries?' And he said, 'No, but as captain of the host of the Lord am I now come.'*" And so he appeared to Gideon (Jdg 6:11ff). and so also to Manoah (Jdg 13:17–21). Here Christ appeared to Manoah in a representation both of his incarnation and death; of his incarnation, in that he appeared in a human form; and of his death and sufferings, represented by the sacrifice of a kid, and by his ascending up in the flame of the sacrifice; intimating, that it was he that was the great sacrifice, that must be offered up to God for a sweet savor, in the fire of his wrath, as that kid was burned and ascended up in the flame. *Thus Christ appeared, time after time, in the form of that nature he was afterwards to assume; because he now appeared on the same design and to carry on the same work.*

Jonathan Edwards (1703-1758)[37]

All the divine appearances of the ancient economy are referred to *one person.*—Compare Gen. 18:2, 17; 28:13; 32:9, 31; Ex. 3:14, 15; 13:21; 20:1, 2; 25:21; Deut. 4:33, 36, 39; Neh. 9:7–28. This one person is called Jehovah, the incommunicable name of God, and at the same time *angel,* or *one sent.*—Compare Gen. 31:11, 13; 48:15, 16; Hosea 12:2, 5. Compare Ex. 3:14, 15, with Acts 7:30–35; and Ex. 13:21, with Ex. 14:19; and Ex. 20:1, 2, with Acts 7:38; Isa. 63:7, 9. But God the Father has been seen by no man (John 1:18; 6:46): neither could he be an angel, or one sent

---

[37] Jonathan Edwards, "A History of the Work of Redemption," in *The Works of Jonathan Edwards*, vol. 1 (Banner of Truth Trust, 1974), 551.

by any other; yet God the Son has been seen (1 John 1:1, 2), and sent (John 5:36).

A. A. Hodge (1823-1886)[38]

(a) The angel of Jehovah identifies himself with Jehovah; (b) he is identified with Jehovah by others; (c) he accepts worship due only to God. Though the phrase "angel of Jehovah" is sometimes used in the later Scriptures to denote a merely human messenger or created angel, it seems in the Old Testament, with hardly more than a single exception, to designate the pre-incarnate Logos, whose manifestations in angelic or human form foreshadowed his final coming in the flesh. (a) Gen. 22:11, 16—"the angel of Jehovah called unto him [Abraham, when about to sacrifice Isaac]... By myself have I sworn, with Jehovah"; 31:11, 13— "the angel of God said unto me [Jacob].... I am the God of Beth-el." (b) Gen. 16:9, 13—"angel of Jehovah said unto her ... and she called the name of Jehovah that spoke unto her, You are a God who sees"; 48:15, 16—"the God who fed me ... the angel who hath redeemed me."

Augustus Strong (1836-1921)[39]

---

[38] A. A. Hodge, *Outlines of Theology: Rewritten and Enlarged* (New York: Hodder & Stoughton, 1878), 170.
[39] Augustus Hopkins Strong, *Systematic Theology* (Philadelphia: American Baptist Publication Society, 1907), 319.

It is another question, however, whether there may
not exist in the pages of the Old Testament turns of
expression or records of occurrences in which one already acquainted with the doctrine of the Trinity may
fairly see indications of an underlying implication of
it. The older writers discovered intimations of the
Trinity in such phenomena as the plural form of the
Divine name Ĕlōhīm, the occasional employment with
reference to God of plural pronouns ("Let us make
man in our image," Gen. 1:26; 3:22; 11:7; Isa. 6:8),
or of plural verbs (Gen. 20:13; 35:7), certain repeti-
tions of the name of God which seem to distinguish
between God and God (Ps. 45:6, 7; 105:1; Hos. 1:7),
threefold liturgical formulas Num. 6:24, 26; Isa. 6:3),
a certain tendency to hypostatize the conception of
Wisdom (Prov. 8), and especially the remarkable phenomena connected with the appearances of the Angel
of Jehovah (Gen. 16:2–13, 22:11, 16; 31:11, 13;
48:15, 16; Ex. 3:2, 4, 5; Jdg. 13:20–22) ... After all is
said, in the light of the later revelation, the Trinitarian
interpretation remains the most natural one of the
phenomena which the older writers frankly inter-
preted as intimations of the Trinity; especially of those
connected with the descriptions of the Angel of Jehovah no doubt.

B. B. Warfield (1851-1921)[40]

[40] Benjamin B. Warfield, *The Works of Benjamin B. Warfield: Biblical Doctrines*, vol. 2 (Bellingham, WA: Logos Bible Software, 2008), 140-41.

God ... visits his people in personal beings ... Among all these envoys of God the Messenger of the Lord (מלאך יהוה) occupies a special place. He appears to Hagar (Gen 16:6–13; 21:17–20); to Abraham (Gen 18; 19; 22; 24:7; 40); to Jacob (Gen 28:13–17; 31:11–13; 32:24–30; cf. Hos 12:4; Gen 48:15, 16); to, and at the time of, Moses (Ex 3:2f.; 13:21; 14:19; 23:20–23; 32:34; 33:2f.; cf. Num 20:16; Isa 63:8, 9; and further also Josh 5:13, 14; Jdg 6:11–24; 13:2–23). This *Malak YHWH* is not an independent symbol nor a created angel but a true personal revelation and appearance of God, distinct from him (Ex 23:20–23; 33:14f.; Isa. 63:8, 9) and still one with him in name (Gen 16:13; 31:13; 32:28, 30; 48:15, 16; Ex 3:2f.; 23:20–23; Jdg 13:3), in power (Gen 16:10, 11; 21:18; 18:14, 18; Ex. 14:19; Jdg 6:21), in redemption and blessing (Gen 48:16; Ex 3:8; 23:20; Isa 63:8, 9), in adoration and honor (Gen 18:3; 22:12; Ex 23:21) ... The angel of the covenant again appears in prophecy (Zech. 1:8–12:3) and will come to his temple (Mal. 3:1). Theophany reaches its climax, however, in Christ who is the (Angel, Glory, Image, Word, Son of God) in whom God is fully revealed and fully given.

Herman Bavinck (1854-1921)[41]

---

[41] Herman Bavinck, John Bolt, and John Vriend, *Reformed Dogmatics: Prolegomena*, vol. 1 (Grand Rapids, MI: Baker Academic, 2003), 328–330.

The most important and characteristic form of revelation in the patriarchal period is that through 'the Angel of Jehovah' or 'the Angel of God'. The references are: Gen. 16:7; 22:11, 15; 24:7, 40; 31:11; 48:16 [cp. also *Hos.* 12:4, with reference to *Gen.* 32:24ff.].

The peculiarity in all these cases is that, on the one hand, the Angel distinguishes himself from Jehovah, speaking of Him in the third person, and that, on the other hand, in the same utterance he speaks of God in the first person. Of this phenomenon various explanations have been offered ... We must assume that behind the twofold representation there lies a real manifoldness in the inner life of the Deity. If the Angel sent were Himself partaker of Godhead, then He could refer to God as his sender, and at the same time speak as God, and in both cases there would be reality behind it. Without this much of what we call the Trinity, the transaction could not but have been unreal and illusory.

Geerhardus Vos (1862-1949)[42]

The mysterious "angel of the LORD" or "angel of God," who appears often in the early Old Testament story and is sometimes identified with the God from whom he is at other times distinguished (Gen. 16:7–13; 18:1–33; 22:11–18; 24:7, 40; 31:11–13; 32:24–

---

[42] Geerhardus Vos, *Biblical Theology: Old and New Testaments* (Eugene, OR: Wipf & Stock Publishers, 2003), 72–73.

30; 48:15–16; Exod. 3:2–6; 14:19; 23:20–23; 32:34–33:5; Num. 22:22–35; Josh. 5:13–15; Judg. 2:1–5; 6:11–23; 9:13–23), is in some sense God acting as his own messenger, and is commonly seen as a preincarnate appearance of God the Son.

J. I. Packer (1926-)[43]

He is the "angel" who redeems us (Gen 48:16). He is not a creaturely angel, but the angel of the Lord with whom Jacob wrestled (32:22–32), a pre-incarnate manifestation of the Messiah, according to churchmen throughout history. Centuries after Jacob lived, God came to earth to defeat sin and reveal His faithfulness (John 1:1–18).

R. C. Sproul (1939-2017)[44]

---

[43] J. I. Packer, *Concise Theology: A Guide to Historic Christian Beliefs* (Wheaton, IL: Tyndale House, 1993), 65.
[44] R. C. Sproul, *Tabletalk Magazine, November 2007: The English Reformation* (Lake Mary, FL: Ligonier Ministries, 2007), 47.

Glossary of Works & Authors Cited

There are many obscure and long since forgotten authors and works cited in Owen's discussion on the Angel. This Glossary is provided to acquaint you with some of them.

ABENEZRA. Abraham ben Meir Ibn Ezra (1089-1167). One of the most distinguished Jewish biblical commentators and philosophers of the Middle Ages.

ABRAHAM SABA (1440-1509). Seba or Sabaa. Portuguese rabbi who wrote a commentary on the Pentateuch called *Tseror Hammor* (*Bundle of Myrrh*; Venice, 1523).

ATHENAGORAS (fl. 176–180). Early Christian philosopher and apologist from Athens, whose only authenticated writing, *A Plea Regarding Christians*, is addressed to the emperors Marcus Aurelius and Commodus, and defends Christians from the common accusations of atheism, incest and cannibalism.

BECHAI (1255-1340). Bahya ben Asher ibn Halawa. Distinguished Spanish rabbi who wrote a commentary on the Hebrew Bible.

BEN UZZIEL (first cent. BC – AD). Pupil of the famed Hillel the Elder, he is authored some of the Targums.

CLEMENT OF ALEXANDRIA (c. 150–215). A highly educated Christian convert from paganism, head of the catechetical school in Alexandria and pioneer of Christian scholarship.

ELIJAH LEVITA (1469-1549). Renaissance Hebrew grammarian, scholar, and poet. Wrote a diction called Tishbi on the Talmud, Midrash, and Targums.

JARKI (1040-1105). Shlomo Yitzchaki, also called Rashi, he was a medieval French rabbi and author of a commentary on the Tanakh.

JONAH (4th century). Palestinian amora rabbi who was the leading rabbinical authority in the 4th amoraic generation.

JUSTIN MARTYR (100/110–165). Palestinian philosopher who was converted to Christianity. He traveled to Rome and wrote several apologies (defenses of the faith) against both pagans and Jews; he was eventually martyred.

MENAHEM BEN BENJAMIN RECANATI (1223-1290). Italian rabbi who wrote a commentary on the Torah.

MOSES BEN NAHMAN (1194-1270). Commonly called Nachmanides or Ramban. Leading medieval Jewish scholar, rabbi, philosopher, physician, kabbalist, and biblical commentator. He lived most of his life in Girona, Catalonia (Spain).

PHILO (20 BC – 50 AD). Alexandrians Jewish Hellenistic philosopher who lived during the time of Christ, he is one of the best monotheistic proponents who believed in a "second God" called the Logos, which lends itself nicely towards an understanding of Christ in the OT.

REUCHLIN, JOHANN (1455-1522). German humanist and Greek and Hebrew scholar. He wrote a treatise *On the Art of Kabbalah* (1517).

TARGUM. A Targum is a paraphrastic rendition of the Hebrew Scripture into Aramaic for Jews who did not speak Hebrew. They contain both oral tradition and interpretation of the Scripture and were probably first written down around the first century by the Jews.

TATIAN (second century). Christian apologist from the East. Famous for his Gospel harmony, the *Diatessaron*, he also wrote *Address to the Greeks*, a defense of Christianity addressed to the pagan world.

TERTULLIAN (c. 155/160–225/250). Carthaginian apologist and polemicist who laid the foundations of Christology and Trinitarian Orthodoxy in the West, though he himself was later estranged from the catholic tradition.

Author Index

Scripture Index

ABOUT THE EDITOR

Doug has pastored the Reformed Baptist Church of Northern Colorado since 2001. He graduated from Bethel College in 1992, majoring in Marketing and minoring in Bible. He was a youth pastor for four years in Denver. He holds the Master of Divinity degree from Denver Seminary (2001).

Doug has served on councils and boards for two Baptist Associations, the current one which he helped found in 2016. The Reformed Baptist Network seeks to glorify God through fellowship and cooperation in fulfilling the Great Commission to the ends of the earth. There are currently 42 churches in this international association of churches.

Doug has co-hosted the radio show Journey's End, the Peeranormal podcast, started the Waters of Creation Publishing Company, owned two small business in Minneapolis, and has appeared on numerous podcasts and radio shows.

Married since 1994, he and Janelle are the proud parents of four beautiful young girls. Born and raised in Colorado, he has climbed all 54 of Colorado's 14,000 ft. mountains and also Mt. Rainier (WA) and Mt. Shasta (CA).

To find out more about any of these things go to:
https://www.dougvandorn.com/

The Church website is
https://rbcnc.com

Books in the Christ In All Scripture Series

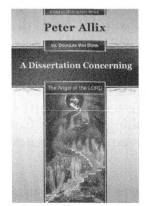

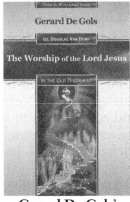

John Owen's treatment is perfect for those wanting to ground their theology of the Angel in the high orthodoxy of the Reformation. The quotations from the Fathers bolster his thesis.

Peter Allix's work is comprehensive and is especially helpful for those familiar with modern scholarship wishing to root their theology in conservative Protestant/Reformed orthodoxy.

Gerard De Gols' study, especially the second half, is imminently practical and would help anyone wanting to learn more about why it matters that Christ is present in the Old Testament.

Owen, Allix, and De Gols together in one volume, minus quotations from the Fathers and Reformers.

The Second Edition of *From the Shadows to the Savior*, it explores even more of the titles given to Christ in the OT than Allix goes into.

Practical sermons are for the further exploration of the fullness of Christ, especially as he is found in the NT.

Other Books by Doug Van Dorn

Giants: Sons of the Gods

The bestselling non-fiction book on Genesis 6 and the Nephilim.
150 reviews. 4.5+++ stars on Amazon.

Goliath. You know the story. But why is it in the Bible? Is it just to give us a little moral pick-me-up as we seek to emulate a small shepherd boy who defeated a giant? Have you ever wondered where Goliath came from? Did you know he had brothers, one with 24 fingers and toes? Did you know their ancestry is steeped in unimaginable horror? Genesis 6. The Nephilim. The first few verses of this chapter have long been the speculation of supernatural events that produced demigods and a flood that God used to destroy the whole world. The whole world remembers them. Once upon a time, all Christians knew them. But for many centuries this view was mocked, though it was the only known view at the time of the writing of the New Testament. Today, it is making a resurgence among Bible-believing scholars, and for good reason. The Nephilim were on the earth in those days, and also afterward...

This book delves deep into the dark and ancient recesses of our past to bring you rich treasures long buried. It is a carefully researched, heavily footnoted, and selectively illustrated story of the giants of the Bible. There is more here than meets the eye, much more. Here you will learn the invisible, supernatural storyline of the Bible that is always just beneath the surface, lurking like the spawn of the ancient leviathan. It is a storyline no person can afford to ignore any longer. Unlike other more sensational books on the topic, there is no undue speculation to be found here. The author is a Bible-believing Christian who refuses to use such ideas to tell you the end of the world is drawing nigh. Once you discover the truth about these fantastic creatures, you will come to see the ministry and work of Jesus Christ in a very new and exalting light. Come. Learn the fascinating, sobering, yet true story of real giants who played a significant role in the bible ... and still do so today.

Available in Paperback or Kindle at Amazon.com

The Unseen Realm: Q & A Companion
Edited by Michael Heiser.
Published by Lexham Press.

In *The Unseen Realm*, Dr. Michael S. Heiser unpacked 15 years of research while exploring what the Bible really says about the supernatural world. That book has nearly 900 reviews and a five-star rating. It is a game-changer

Doug helps you further explore *The Unseen Realm* with a fresh perspective and an easy-to-follow format. The book summarizes key concepts and themes from Heiser's book and includes questions aimed at helping you gain a deeper understanding of the biblical author's supernatural worldview.

The format is that of a catechism: A Question followed by the Answer. There are 95 Questions (nod to Martin Luther) divided into 12 Parts:

Part I—God
Part II—The Lesser Gods
Part III—The Sons of God
Part IV—Divine Council
Part V—Sin, Rebellion, and the Fall
Part VI—Rebellion before the flood
Part VII—Rebellion after the flood
Part VIII—The Promise Anticipated
Part IX—The Promise Fulfilled
Part X—The Good News

Available in Paperback or Kindle at Amazon.com or on the Bible-software platform Logos at Logos.com

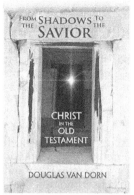

From the Shadows to the Savior:
Christ in the Old Testament

Few subjects are as important--yet ignored or misapplied--as the one addressed in this book. Jesus Christ is the absolute center and focus of the totality of God's word. Many people confess this belief, since Jesus himself taught it (Luke 24:27; John 5:39). Christians have done well to see this on one or two levels, yet truly understanding just how primary he is as an actor—even in the Old Testament—is something few have considered.

In this book, adapted from a series of blog posts for the Decablog, Doug helps us see the light of Christ that emerges from the dark hallways of Scriptures that so many find outdated, unintelligible, and irrelevant for today's Church.

Learn how Christ is found in such things as prophecy, typology, and the law. Then, come in for a deeper study of how the Person himself is actually present, walking, speaking, and acting, beginning in the very first book of the Bible. Learn how words such as "Word," "Name," "Glory," and "Wisdom" are all ideas that the Scripture itself attaches to Christ who in the OT is called The Angel of the LORD. Then see if such ideas don't radically change the way you think about all of God's word in this truly life-changing summary of Christ in the Old Testament.

Chapters:
NT Passages and Reflections
Christ in Prophecy
Christ in Typology
Christ and the Law
Christ: The Angel of the LORD
Christ: The Word of God
Christ: The Name of the LORD
Christ: The Wisdom of God
Christ: The Son of God
Christ: The Glory of God
Christ: The Right Arm of God

Available in Paperback or Kindle at Amazon.com

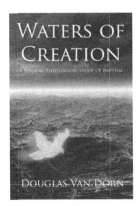

Waters of Creation:
A Biblical-Theological Study of Baptism

This is the one book on baptism that you must read. It was seven years in the making. Doug believes that until a new approach is taken, separations over the meaning, mode, and recipients of baptism will never be bridged.

This new approach traces the roots of baptism deep into the OT Scriptures. When understood properly, we discover that baptism is always the sign that God has used to initiate his people into a new creation. Baptism in the NT is not "new." Rather, it derives its origin from OT predecessors. It has a direct, sacramental counterpart, and it isn't circumcision. It is baptism. When we understand that baptism comes from baptism, especially in its sacramental expression in the priestly covenant, reasons for the NT practice begin to make perfect sense.

Now Baptists have an argument that infant Baptists can finally understand, because we are beginning our argument in the same place. This is an Old Testament covenantal approach to the Baptist position with baptistic conclusions as to the mode and recipients of baptism. That's what happens when we root baptism in baptism rather than circumcision.

Chapters:
The Baptism of Jesus
Baptism and the Sanctuary
Baptism and the Priesthood
Baptism and the Covenant
Implications for Christian Baptism

Available in Paperback or Kindle at Amazon.com

Covenant Theology:
A Reformed Baptist Primer

Covenant theology is often said to be the domain of infant Baptists alone. But there really are such things as Reformed Baptists who believe in covenant theology as a basic system for approaching Scripture.

This primer sets out to give the basics of a Reformed Baptist covenant theology and to do so in a way that is understandable to the uninitiated. It was originally a series we did on Sunday nights at our church. It agrees with classical formulations of covenant theology in that there is a Covenant of Redemption, a Covenant of Works, and a Covenant of Grace in the Bible.

The book takes a multi-perspective approach to the Covenant of Redemption in that this covenant is the basis for the classic formula that Christ's death is sufficient for all, but efficient for the elect. It sees the Covenant of Works for Adam in a broader context of a covenant made with all of creation, a covenant where laws establish the parameters for creation's existence.

It differs from Paedobaptist covenant theology in that it sees the Covenant of Grace as only properly coming through Jesus Christ. OT gracious covenants are typological of the Covenant of Grace but save people on the basis of the coming work of Christ through faith alone. This is the traditional way Reformed Baptists have articulated the Covenant of Grace.

Finally, it sees an entire covenant in the Old Testament as often (but not always) missing from formulations of covenant theology. In the opinion of the author, this "priestly covenant" is vital to a proper understanding of 1. The continuity of the practice of baptism from OT to NT, 2. The answer to why we never find infants being baptized in the NT, and 3. A more precise way to parse the legal aspects of the OT economy, thereby helping us understand why the moral law continues today. This volume works from the basic presupposition that continuity in God's word is more basic than discontinuity. In this, it differs from dispensationalism and new covenant theology. The book suggests that this is the greatest strength of covenant theology, which does also recognize discontinuity.

Available in Paperback or Kindle at Amazon.com

Galatians:
A Supernatural Justification

A play on words, the subtitle of this book gives you the two main points it tries to get across. Galatians central message teaches how a person is *justified* before a holy God. This once precious and central teaching of Protestant theology is often misunderstood or relegated the pile of irrelevant, stale doctrine.

Perhaps that is why the Apostle Paul supercharges his teaching with an oft-overlooked side of this letter - the *supernatural* beings who tempt us and teach us to give up the only truth that will save us. Galatian Christians would have been familiar with these supernatural beings; their culture was steeped in it. Thus, they mistake Paul for the messenger-healer god Hermes, and Barnabas for Zeus. Paul's warning: "Even if we or an angel from heaven should preach to you a gospel contrary to the one we preached to you, let him be accursed." This is Paul's fatherly way of showing his children in the faith that the gospel is paramount; it alone is able to save. Such a warning like this can have new power, as people are returning with reckless abandon to the worship of the old gods.

This book is from a series of sermons preached at the Reformed Baptist Church of Northern Colorado in 2011.

Available in Paperback or Kindle at Amazon.com

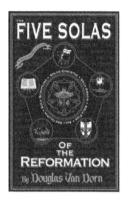

The Five Solas
of the Reformation

The 500th anniversary of the Reformation occurred in 2017. It was October 31, 1517 that Martin Luther nailed his 95 Thesis to the door of the great cathedral at Wittenberg, Germany. He had no idea what that simple act would do. His bold proclamation and challenge to for Rome to reform her ways and beliefs was met with hostility from some and great sympathy from others. Out of this sympathy arose Protestantism, a movement deeply concerned with grounding all things on Holy Scripture, giving glory to God alone, and recovering for that generation the biblical gospel of Jesus Christ. In five chapters, Doug Van Dorn takes us back to these ancient catchphrases that once moved a continent. Scripture Alone, Grace Alone, Faith Alone, Christ Alone, and To God Be the Glory Alone became the rallying cry of all who longed to see men and women, boys and girls saved and set free from sin, death, and the devil. The end of the book contains four helpful Appendices on songs, Church Fathers on the solas, a bibliography for further research, and a letter from Martin Luther.

Available in Paperback or Kindle at Amazon.com

Made in the USA
Columbia, SC
26 December 2024

50683880R00063